A REQUIEM
FOR THE RENASCENCE

A REQUIEM FOR THE RENASCENCE

*The State of Fiction
in the
Modern South*

WALTER SULLIVAN

*MERCER UNIVERSITY LAMAR
MEMORIAL LECTURES, NO. 18*

THE UNIVERSITY OF GEORGIA PRESS

ATHENS

Library of Congress Catalog Card Number: 75–21176
International Standard Book Number: 0–8203–0390–9

The University of Georgia Press, Athens 30602

Set in 11 on 15 pt. Mergenthaler Baskerville
Printed in the United States of America

"Myth" appeared in the *Southern Review*, volume 11 (1975).

For
Ward Allen
and
Virgil LeQuire

This small memento
after more than twenty years.

Contents

Foreword

A REQUIEM FOR THE RENASCENCE IS, IN WALTER SULLIVAN'S words, "an effort to find . . . the end in the beginning, though one may despair of discovering a beginning in the end." Professor Sullivan discovers in the cultural and moral conditions under which the southern renascence began in the twenties the reasons for its demise in the fifties. The southern community and the myth which sustained it had to be dying but not yet completely dead in order for the renascence to occur, but finally the death of the myth and the community meant the death of the renascence as well.

In proposing that the renascence is over, that only requiems can be sung for it now, Professor Sullivan continues the dialogue in which he and Louis D. Rubin, Jr., have been principal spokesmen. Indeed, *A Requiem for the Renascence* is of a piece with the two Lamar lectures in literature which preceded it, Professor Rubin's *The Writer in the South: Studies in a Literary Community* and Lewis P. Simpson's *The Dispossessed Garden: Pastoral and History in Southern Literature*, delivered in 1971 and 1973, respectively. All three lecturers are concerned with the relation-

ship of the serious southern writer to his community and
to southern and American myth.

Professor Sullivan, like his predecessors, is superbly
lucid and persuasive in his readings of individual works of
literature. In his generalizations, he is openly and admira-
bly a moralist, who calls literary artists to provide us access
to the meaning that lies in human experience, and whose
readings of literature illuminate the possibilities of our
gaining such access. His healthy faith informs his work
and reverberates throughout it.

When Mrs. Eugenia Dorothy Blount Lamar established the endowment which maintains Mercer University's Lamar Memorial Lectures, she sought to encourage
and support scholarship which would continually focus
attention on the values of southern culture. When Walter
Sullivan delivered his lectures at Mercer, he brought us
not only his extraordinarily gracious personality and the
vigorous and radiant presence of Mrs. Sullivan, but also
the important contribution to the study of southern values
which this book represents. We are very grateful.

> Michael Cass
> For the Lamar Lectures Committee

Mercer University
Macon, Georgia

Preface

FOR MORE THAN A DECADE I HAVE BEEN ARGUING THAT THE southern literary renascence ended with World War II, and the lectures published here are a continuation of that theme. I have attempted some slight redefinitions of those attributes of southern society that furnished the basis for the renascence, and I have tried to trace cultural changes, most of them for the worse in my judgment, which have in turn deprived southern writing of any proper foundations on which to stand. To state the matter so bluntly is to make a pessimistic advertisement for the essays that follow, and I must in all honesty acknowledge the general gloominess of my point of view. But I do not despair. Our solution, as I conceive it, is to transcend the past and the present by a pursuit of values that are metaphysical and therefore eternal. And this will require a revaluation of the role of the artist in the contemporary world.

Though the errors and barbarisms to be found here are solely and distinctly mine, I wish to thank Professor Gerhart Niemeyer, who many years ago introduced me to the works of Eric Voegelin and Mircea Eliade; their brilliant analyses of the historical process and the human situation have helped to engender many of the ideas in this small book. I am grateful also to George Core, who is ever willing to read and comment upon one more manuscript imposed upon him by his friends. I commend Kenneth Cherry of the Georgia Press for his help and patience, and I thank particularly the two gentlemen to whom this book is dedicated for the hours they spent with me loitering in Confederate cemeteries and brooding beside bullet-scarred walls. Together we took our apparently aimless and highly personal excursion into the past, and for reasons that I have not attempted to examine, the memory of those times came back to me strongly while I was writing and delivering these lectures.

Being in Macon in November is a pleasure in itself. Our stay—for my wife was with me—was enhanced by the gracious hospitality of the Mercer community. Jane and I are particularly grateful to Spencer and Caroline King, to Michael and Lynn Cass, to Kenneth and Jo Hammond of the Mercer faculty; to Cynthia and Herbert Birdsey, the latter a trustee of the Lamar lecture series; and to Claire and Dick Dodd of Marshallville, at whose house we had lunch one memorable day. As always Jane has borne my bad disposition and shared the agony of this work, and as always it is to her that I am most grateful.

Walter Sullivan

Vanderbilt University

Introduction

THE STUDY OF LITERATURE IS FRAUGHT WITH UNCERTAINTY. There is the question of achievement—whether the new writers are as good as those of the preceding generation. And one must deal with the old mystery which surrounds the relationship of a writer to the culture which produces him. Certainly writers are born, as the saying goes, but they are also made by the civilization in which they find themselves. Otherwise all the great ages of literature would have to be explained as simple confluences of genetic accident—a solution that would strain the law of averages and deny arbitrarily what many scholars have worked diligently and convincingly to prove. Yet the relationship *is* mysterious, and what may be said concerning it is speculative at best.

Perhaps I can be more positive if I briefly cover some old familiar ground. Southern regional fiction is said to have risen out of the folk tradition, out of the southern penchant for telling tales and creating myths, out of the land and man's closeness to it, and out of a fundamentalist cosmic view. Concerning regionalism and community W. B. Yeats put the case to James Joyce this way:

The artist, when he has lived for a long time in his own mind with the example of other artists as deliberate as himself, gets into a world of ideas pure and simple. He becomes very highly individualized and at last by sheer pursuit of perfection becomes sterile. Folk imagination on the other hand creates endless images of which there are no ideas. Its stories . . . are successions of pictures like those seen by children in the fire. . . . In the towns . . . you don't find what old writers used to call the people; you find instead a few highly cultivated, highly perfected individual lives, and great multitudes who imitate them and cheapen them. You find, too, . . . an impulse towards creation which grows gradually weaker and weaker. In the country . . . you find people who are hardly individualized to any great extent. They live through the same round of duty and they think about life and death as their fathers have told them, but in speech, in the telling of tales, in all that has to do with the play of imagery, they have an endless abundance. . . . Everything seems possible to them, and because they can never be surprised, they imagine the most surprising things.[1]

By now what Yeats says seems too obvious to require supporting evidence, and the same is true of the numerous commentaries on southern regionalism and the sense of place by Louis Rubin, Robert Heilman, Richard Weaver, Frederick Hoffman, and many other critics. We have been told that the traditional southerner as human being and as artist was wary of utopian schemes; that he believed in the flawed nature of man; that he considered, in Weaver's words, "the whole [of life's experience] . . . greater than the analyzable parts."[2] Again and again it is pointed out that he was pious, which means, I take it, that he thought the universe to be ordered by a transcendent and in the highest sense mysterious force.

In our day of disorder and faltering belief, one is tempted to try to explain not only the southern renascence, but previous literary accomplishments as well in terms of this last mentioned traditional notion—a faith in and relationship to an omnipotent God. I suspect that with a little finesse one could make a fairly reasonable case for the thesis that all Western literature for the last two thousand years has been dependent on and shaped by the Christian ambience. Writers who were themselves Christians had a ready-made moral framework in which their characters might maneuver, a source of symbol and image, and even, as in Trollope, a ground for plots. They enjoyed the security of knowing who they were and where they were supposed to be going spiritually and what life, on its highest plane, entails. I would not minimize these endowments: it is a distinct advantage for a writer to be able to accept St. Thomas's proof of existence, and thereby be freed of the burden of proving it in his own work. Much modern literature will demonstrate the sad fact that some of the questions that are most basic to philosophy turn out to be peripheral and dead when they are transplanted into literature. Fiction takes its first life from human beings, not from ideas.

For those writers who were not Christian, there was always the establishment to react against. It is reported that James Joyce once reprimanded a biographer for referring to him as a Catholic by remarking, "For the sake of precision and to get the correct contour on me, you ought to allude to me as a Jesuit."[3] The impish truth behind this joke has many ramifications. But in point of fact it is difficult to believe that Joyce's work would not have been grievously impoverished had he not had the church to defy. In Ernest Hemingway's fiction, the priest is a kind of initiate: Jake Barnes wishes he weren't such a rotten Catholic, and the old Count Greffi longs to be *croyant*. Even in *La Peste* the bishop with his refrain of man's guilt and God's punishment is necessary to set off the existentialist answer and to make Camus's representation of the absurd world complete.

One suspects that this argument works as well as it does because Christianity has been the dominant theological and cultural force in the Western world for the last two millennia. The flaws of this thesis—for instance the flowering of literature before Christ and the remarkable fertility of Jewish writing in our own time and others—are obvious. Fiction is a moral art, which is to say it deals with moral problems and puts its characters into situations of moral significance; but its allegiance is to the natural law, that system of belief in right and wrong which is common to men and societies of whatever persuasion. When the natural law, or a great part of it, is embodied in a traditional culture, as it was in the South, the writer may agree or not with that law and the shared belief of his community; but he is likely to be delivered from a fatal error. He will see life for the complex thing that it is: he will not oversimplify the human condition.

This mistake of seeing the world as ultimately fathomable, ultimately manageable, and therefore ultimately simple has been a fault of men from the beginning of time, and consequently a fault of kings and of parliaments, of theologians, and of writers. I take the Midas fable to be a commentary on this theme; the Christian inquisitions to be historical manifestations of it. Our own technological age, which has solved many of the ancient riddles, is particularly vulnerable. There is no need to labor this point. The humanist who once drew his wisdom from Aristotle and Sophocles, Virgil and Shakespeare now puts his faith in Marx and Freud, in David Riesman and B. F. Skinner. That is to say, in plans of action that guarantee the perfection of the world.

Life is change, and history teaches that the moment of perfection, or the closest approach to that moment for any civilization, is the beginning of decline. Literature is likely to flourish in the first and almost imperceptible period of decay; but it is no more immune to erosion than any other human institution. Thus after the English renascence, the interregnum, and the death of Milton, there were the political satires and the voluminous criticism, proper accompaniment to the long struggle between Whig and Tory and the Jacobean plots. So does our own renascence diminish as our civilization fitfully attempts to redefine and fulfill itself.

It seems to me that the death of the culture which produced the southern renascence, the decline of regionalism itself as reality and therefore as literary source, has been portrayed in fiction at least twice: by William Faulkner in the Snopes trilogy and by Andrew Lytle in *The Velvet Horn*. The Snopes books, viewed as a whole, must be unique in all literature in their juxtaposition of genius and folly: they show Faulkner at his best and at his worst. Flem Snopes in *The Hamlet* is not only the scourge of Frenchman's Bend, the unworthy successor to Sartorises and Compsons, the incipient aristocrat of the new materialistic view; but he is the eternal enemy of every humane society; he is a manifestation of the avarice that infects us all. But as late as 1940 Faulkner retained hope about southern society. One theme of *The Hamlet* is the victory of Snopesism, but another equally important theme is man's fidelity and his capacity to love. Labove, who has struggled to get off the farm, is willing to return to it for the love of Eula. Jack Houston comes back from Texas to marry Lucy Pate and then is inconsolably grieved by her death. Mink Snopes's incontinent wife, whom he found in the lumber camp, stays with him in spite of his brutality and crime. And at the end of the action Mrs. Armstid is taking food to her crazy husband, whose cupidity has ruined them both. Even the idiot Ike, an innocent in the old sense, loves the cow, but loves selflessly, and thereby points the way to man's possible restoration. In its rich ambiguity the novel is optimistic, even triumphant: enduring man is almost a match for original sin, and in this sense he will prevail.

One could wish that Faulkner had stopped here. The end is apparent. The white man has corrupted himself with his own greed as surely and as tragically as he corrupted the Indians with it a century earlier. Hope does remain, and it is a valid hope, for it is rooted not in some vague notion of generic humanity, but in obstinate, exasperating, infinitely complex individual men and women of all ages and sizes and persuasions and colors. Stubborn and guilty, but idealistic and even heroic too, they hold the world together. In the midst of flux they help us cling to what is good.

In his last years Faulkner abandoned his own vision. As Peter Swiggart suggests (and as is apparent in his correspondence with Malcolm Cowley), he seems to have discovered that he was writing a southern chronicle. He became self-conscious in his regionalism to the detriment of his art. "In *The Town* and *The Mansion*," Swiggart writes, "Faulkner deprives himself of strong backdrop events through his effort to create a realistic social environment. His rational witnesses are treated more sympathetically and magnified in importance. But at the same time they are deprived of anything very interesting, to themselves and to the reader, to think and speculate about. The result is a writing impasse that the author tries to escape principally through rhetorical means."[4] Or, one might add, he tries to escape through a new commitment to the social and political clichés of our time.

"It should be obvious that polemics is one discipline and fiction another," Andrew Lytle has said. "If you are going to preach, get into the pulpit; if you want to bring about political reforms, run for office; social reforms, behave yourself and mind your manners. . . . When a novel obviously makes an appeal other than its proper aesthetic one, you may be sure it has been written with the left hand."[5] How, in this time of grave social crisis, does the southern writer, who is also a southern citizen, avoid being polemical? Lytle has shown us such behavior, too, in *The Velvet*

Horn. I take one theme of this remarkable novel to be the decay of the traditional southern civilization. Lytle does not pursue this in terms of abstractions: instead he writes of family responsibility and man's relationship to his neighbor, of nature defiled and individual human guilt. Speaking of his own spilling blood, the dying Jack Cropleigh says, "It will leave a stain worth all the books."[6] So it will, for so it has throughout all history. One man's dying, which is to say one man's courage, is better than a thousand speeches or theories or essays in explanation and defense. At the end of the novel Lucius, having sought out the truth about his birth, assumes his own guilt which is inseparable from the guilt of his father. His atonement is private and sacramental, manifested in his marriage to Ada Belle.

The Velvet Horn seems to have been one of the last successful novels depicting what Allen Tate has deemed "the opposition of an heroic myth to the secularization of man in our age."[7] It is no coincidence, I think, that both Lytle and Faulkner see the destruction of the South as having properly got underway in the 1890s. None of the new traditionalists—to use John Bradbury's term from *Renaissance in the South*—was born close enough to that era to write about it convincingly or to understand it properly. And with each passing year subtleties fade, complexities are eradicated by the hardening lines of social conflict. Whether or not we are also beset by a general moral deterioration, the old certainties of right and wrong no longer support us. We are obsessed with group ethics, group action; and as Eric Voegelin has so brilliantly pointed out, a group, any group, has at best a kind of secondary reality. Only nature and man have primary existence, and only man himself, as individual, has will, responsibility, and a partial capacity to damn or save himself.

Southern writers have reacted to the pressures of our torn society in various ways. Some have accepted it and tried to portray it on its own terms. I think, for example, of Carson McCullers. Few fictions have started so well and ended so badly as *Clock Without Hands*. The human values which are captured in the existentialist beginning are subordinated to the argument, subverted by the cause the novel is asked to serve. That the cause should be one that has possessed the American mind like no other since prohibition is of no consequence: nor is it significant that the late Miss McCullers took what most intellectuals and divines feel to be the side of the angels. "Poetry," W. H. Auden wrote in "In Memory of W. B. Yeats," "makes nothing happen." Poetry and prose that attempt to make something happen are, Lytle pointed out, doomed to failure. I can conceive of a good novel, even a great novel, which might be written about human beings caught up in the turmoil of the race question when our present agony is past, and therefore no longer oversimplified by the call for immediate action. But if one disregards such books as *Absalom, Absalom!*, which was written in the thirties and which is, properly speaking, about innocence and pride, I know of no contemporary novel about the race problem which is likely to survive. Yet, whatever his own views, the writer is badgered by critics and public to speak to the issues. For example, a reviewer of a recent southern novel said, "The narrative is swift and clear. It is a handsome and entertaining novel. . . . The characters come alive."[8] But the book was roundly condemned in the end. Its single fault: it did not deal with the problem of segregation. (Indeed Floyd Watkins has demonstrated this point in *The Death of Art*—that propaganda has undermined the southern novel since 1954.)

If the novelist can find strength to turn away from the social tempest, there are other roads open to him, but each is likely to limit his scope. Like Peter Taylor in his best short fiction he may find an aspect of the tradition that has not before been fully exploited and which because of its special and somewhat circumscribed nature remains literarily viable. Or like Madison Jones he may cling sternly to the regionalism of his forebears. Or like Flannery O'Connor he may recast the old material in the mould of dogmatic theology. Or like William Styron he may use the South merely as setting, a place charmingly eccentric and redolent with decadent associations, but in the end no better than any other location for portraying the decline of all civilization, the encroaching bleakness of the human heart.

Taylor seems at once so fresh and so anachronistic that he offers little ground for generalization. His vision resembles that of an old maid aunt endowed with angelic powers of perception. The ramifications of family, the nuances of domestic frictions and affections—many of them profound—are his stock in trade. His ear for a particular kind of dialogue, his ability to describe a girl's clothes or the pattern in bedroom wallpaper are uncanny.

It once seemed that Peter Taylor would be the only American of his generation whose work could stand comparison with that of Frank O'Connor and Chekhov and Joyce. But Taylor has remained essentially a writer of short stories, and since the publication of "Miss Leonora When Last Seen" in 1960 his work has sagged markedly. He will not give us an *Absalom, Absalom!* or an *All the King's Men* or a *Velvet Horn.*

Between Jones and Styron, Styron seems more polished, more sophisticated, more wise in the mores of the broad world. But as a writer he exists in a kind of limbo, cut off from his tradition and unable to find any other, obligated to return home occasionally, but ignorant as to what such returns might signify. He can postulate most interesting and, it would seem, most significant dramatic situations. But his endings are disappointing: they lead nowhere, they show us nothing. Even as existentialist he is a failure: the best he can say to us is that on whatever terms of guilt or error, it is better to live than to die.

Jones on the other hand has a ferocious tenacity. He knows always the grim course that he intends to travel, and he follows it without pity, demonstrating at every turn the decline of traditional values which has set loose anew the devil in men's hearts. His work never fails to amount to something, and his power is unquestionably great. I think he is the best traditionalist of the younger generation, and this is saying a great deal. But I long for a little tenderness, some good along with all the stark and compelling evil, and it is not there. It is not there, I think, not because it no longer in truth exists, though admittedly in our time virtue is often difficult to discover. Instead it would seem that in an increasingly modernized society simply maintaining the old regionalist posture becomes more and more burdensome. Against the contemporary heresy of man's perfectibility one is perhaps obligated to overstate the opposite traditional view.

Flannery O'Connor is probably the best of all southern writers of her generation and after, and her achievement is remarkable in many ways. For one thing she is able to employ Catholic theology as a basis for her fiction without casting her stories and novels in theological terms. Her people are usually Protestants or unbelievers, and their lack of understanding of the laws of God—which continue to operate whether one believes in them or not—contributes to her usual effect of comic irony, an irony that is undergirded by a deadly serious moral view. Like Dickens Miss O'Connor created characters so artistically overdrawn that they gain an added measure of reality through exaggeration and distortion. Her eye for detail never failed her, and because her strange backgrounds are described with absolute circumstantiality, we believe in the places she wrote about and the things she says. But she died young and her canon is small.

I shall use texts from some of the writers that I have discussed here and from others whom I have not mentioned to advance my arguments concerning myth and community and the future of writing in the South.

A REQUIEM
FOR THE RENASCENCE

ONE

Myth

AT THIS LATE DATE IT IS IMPOSSIBLE FOR ONE TO ENTER into a discussion of the literature of the South without experiencing a strong sense of déjà vu. The literary history has been written and rewritten time and again. The works, both major and minor, have been subjected to intense scrutiny and in the realms of both cultural theory and critical judgment, general areas of consensus have been achieved. We know that the South was agrarian, homogeneous, given—to use Allen Tate's famous figure —to looking at and seeing the whole horse, not the fragments of its various manifestations.[1] Before the Civil War the defense of slavery engendered a southern obsession with politics to the extent that little energy remained for literary endeavor. There was Poe; there was Simms, but there were few other writers of even minor significance. The war and its aftermath gave the South a unique history—a unique common experience, and common hardships and a common sense of loss enshrined the tradition of southern romanticism in all its good and bad manifestations and codified the southern attitude toward itself and toward the world at large. All this, and more, has been widely discussed and fully documented and requires no elaboration from me.

We know too, as many critics, including my old friend and colleague Donald Davidson, who gave the first Lamar lectures, have made clear—that the southern renascence like many other great literary movements came into fruition at the moment when the South turned its vision outward and began to seek its destiny under rubrics that governed other sections of the country. Davidson put it this way: "Greece in the fifth century B.C., Rome of the late republic, Italy in Dante's time, England in the sixteenth century, all give us examples of traditional societies invaded by changes that threw them slightly out of balance without at first achieving cultural destruction. The invasion seems always to force certain individuals into an examination of their total inheritance that perhaps they would not otherwise have undertaken. They begin to compose literary works in which the whole metaphysic of the society suddenly takes dramatic or poetic or fictional form."[2] Thus according to Davidson—and almost all other southern literary theorists—the tension and nostalgia and even uncertainty which accompany the twilight of the old southern culture furnished the ground in which the southern literary renascence took root. I have in the past referred to this notion—not entirely facetiously—as the gotterdammerung theory of southern literature,[3] and scholars are in essential agreement concerning its pantheon. Faulkner stands first, but clustered around and near him are any number of others whose names are familiar in almost any company: novelists Wolfe, Warren, Welty, Katherine Anne Porter, and many others; poets Tate, Ransom, Davidson, Warren again, and more. What remains for critics to study and argue about is the necrology of this impressive literary movement: the time of its death and the causes from which it died. Of course this will take us back once more to some of the old material in an effort to find, in Eliot's phrase, the end in the beginning, though one may despair of discovering a beginning in the end.

I want to look first at "Old Mortality" by Katherine Anne Porter. This is a consummately beautiful novella, almost fully realized in every particular, but my specific interest in it is that it deals directly with two themes that are central to the theory I hope to develop: family and myth. You will remember that "Old Mortality" is a striking example of the sophisticated use of point of view. Technically it derives from the eighteenth-century masters of the epistolary novel and from Laurence Sterne in the way that it gives disparate interpretations of the same material glimpsed through different eyes. But it is absolutely modern—think of *All the King's Men*, for example—in its refusal to settle for a single hero; Miss Porter balances one set of actions, one set of themes against another. The dramatic values of the story are developed out of the tension that grows between the two little girls—Maria and Miranda—and their dead Aunt Amy around whom the rest of the family has built a myth.

From the first line the work proceeds with scrupulous honesty. We know—and the girls, though quite young, suspect—that Amy cannot have been as beautiful and accomplished as her brothers and mother and cousins assert. Against the claim that her photograph does not do her justice and the repeated admonitions that whatever talents others may have, Amy's were greater stands the plain fact that the family is given to prevarication. "There were never any fat women in the family, thank God,"[4] the girls' father says early in the narrative, and immediately Maria and Miranda think of two notoriously obese aunts to refute this claim. Still Harry, the father, sees what he wants to see, and by general consent the legend of Amy is allowed to burgeon, immune from cavil or dispute.

Indeed Amy has done her part. However beautiful she was, she was rebellious, wearing a plunging neckline in defiance of her father, cutting her hair to chastise her lover, making the same lover, poor Gabriel, dress in a shepherd's costume that she might better display herself at the masked ball and there betray him. She suffered from tuberculosis and thus languished in bed, her eyes bright with fever, or rose to the detriment of her health to ride for a lark into Mexico with Harry. If we do not read very carefully, we are likely to believe that Gabriel ruined himself for her, for he is cut out of his grandfather's will, but probably this would have happened anyway. Whether Amy ever loved Gabriel, we do not know, for her marriage was a star-crossed affair: her single letter home speaks of loneliness, and six weeks after the wedding she is dead. This is the stuff of the myth on which the girls are raised.

The difference between appearance and reality, the search for the kind of pure human truth that is always so difficult to find, is a theme that appears frequently in Katherine Anne Porter's best fiction: in "Pale Horse, Pale Rider" and "Noon Wine" and in many of the shorter stories. There is always a correcting view, and the antidote to the romantic Amy of part 1 is Gabriel of part 2, grown middle-aged and paunchy and redolent of whisky. The girls, now fourteen and ten, meet him for the first time on one of his good days. Obviously he has been down on his luck, but on this afternoon a mare he owns wins a race and enters the paddock with blood flecking her nostrils. Gabriel has married again after Amy's death, and he takes the girls and their father to visit Miss Honey. She is living in a room at a cheap hotel, and she does not even pretend to be glad to see Amy's brother Harry. Nor will she be cheered by Gabriel's good news, so deeply has her disposition been scarred by their mercurial fortunes.

A final version of the myth appears in part 3. Coming home for Gabriel's funeral, Miranda, now married and because of this estranged from her father, meets her cousin Eva on the train. Eva's chin recedes, her teeth protrude; she has spent her youth seated against the wall while in the middle of the floor boys paid court to her beautiful cousin. Now reconciled to her homeliness and her maiden state, she fights for woman's suffrage, but even death has not softened her resentment against Amy. "It was just sex," Eva says, "their minds dwelt on nothing else."[5] Amy doctored herself with home remedies in an effort to suspend her natural functions. In her shameless pursuit of men she refused to care for her health, and perhaps Amy's quick wedding and early death were not as

innocent as they looked. Eva hints at a premarital liaison
with a man named Raymond. Of course it is another myth,
and Miranda recognizes it as such: "This is no more true
than what I was told before. It's every bit as romantic," she
thinks.[6]

The story ends on a curious, and to some critics, a faulty
note. At the station, Miranda is greeted coldly by her
unforgiving father. Then Harry turns to Eva. She takes
his arm, and while Miranda, an outcast, tags along behind,
these two survivors of the age of Amy plunge back into the
past and the myth that Gabriel helped to create. The
miseries of Eva's childhood seem suddenly to be forgotten. On his side Harry makes a joke of Eva's feminist
activism. In the face of death which is claiming members
of their generation with regularity now, they bury their
differences, moderate their distinct versions of the myth
in their common blood.

Miranda turns away pondering her separation from her
father and Eva, the abyss that she feels opening up between the generations. She is deeply conscious of her
isolation, but the meaning of it eludes her. She gropes for
knowledge, for a stand to take, for the meaning of the
scene that she is living through; she seeks a context within
which to pursue her life, a frame within which to order her
experiences. The passage is too long to quote in its en-
tirety, but even Miranda's repudiation of the myths by
which Eva and her father live is hedged at the last by
ambiguity.

> What is the truth, she asked herself as intently as if the
> question had never been asked, the truth, even about the

smallest, the least important of all the things I must find out? and where shall I begin to look for it? Her mind closed stubbornly against remembering, not the past but the legend of the past, other people's memory of the past, at which she had spent her life peering in wonder like a child at a magic-lantern show. Ah, but there is my own life to come yet, she thought, my own life now and beyond. I don't want any promises, I won't have any false hopes, I won't be romantic about myself. I can't live in their world any longer, she told herself. . . . Let them tell their stories to each other. Let them go on explaining how things happened. . . . At least I can know the truth about what happens to me, she assured herself silently, making a promise to herself, in her hopefulness, her ignorance.[7]

It is hard for us to know how Miss Porter means for us to regard Miranda in this passage. Are we to see her as an innocent whose only trouble is youth, a child, in spite of her marriage, who will understand more and become more like her elders as the years pass? Or is she a daughter of the modern world, already liberated far beyond Eva's dream of the ballot, who is declaring her separation from the institutions of the past without knowing what the future holds in store for her? Or is the ambiguity intended? Are we to be kept in doubt because Miranda herself does not know? It is not my purpose to adjudicate these questions, except in a special sense: to see the end of the story as an image of the southern literary renascence.

Look at the narrative this way. The family is a microcosmic representation of southern society. Fragmented in many ways, distressed by enmities and failures—Eva's jealousy, Amy's selfishness, Gabriel's profligacy—the family nonetheless holds together because of the willingness of its individual members to subordinate their own feelings to the unity it represents. Or, to put the matter more specifically, the family commands a transcendent fidelity, not because of what it actually is but because of the myth which sustains it. To be sure, Amy was loved for herself and because she was loved, her memory is revered. But of more importance she is the heroine of the myth, partially made by her, partially created by the family out of their need for just such a paradigm. In reality the family is like any other: it is comprised of the beautiful and the ugly, the good and the bad, the competent and the ungainly. Left to itself, with no image to worship or example to follow, it would disintegrate against the simple irascibility of flawed mankind. But for a long time at least it is held together by the legend of Amy.

My conclusion, then, is clear and I need not dwell on it. Eva is that familiar figure which we see more and more often these days—the guilt ridden southerner. She sees the faults in her own tradition; she works to remedy some of the wrongs that the tradition has perpetuated. But like Quentin Compson in *Absalom, Absalom!* she can protest with at least some honesty that she does not hate the South,[8] and she is an example of the rich ambiguity that we find in the best creations of southern novelists. Eva at once is destroyer and victim: the myth has shaped her and she cannot fully turn away from it, even as she works to bring it down. Miranda, as we know, is Katherine Anne Porter, caught in this pregnant moment of history. She is at once a part of the old order and apart from it. She loves it, but it has hurt her, for it has rejected her in a way that even Eva has not been rejected. Miranda sees the glory and the doom.

So much then, momentarily at least, for "Old Mortality." There are other embodiments of the southern myth that I wish to consider and the first of these is Thomas Sutpen and his story. *Absalom, Absalom!* is one of the most southern of all novels and one of Faulkner's masterpieces. I have pointed out elsewhere that Sutpen comes very close to being a tragic hero in the truest sense of the term.[9] He is drawn larger than life; he follows a single burning ambition; he is brought down by the design he seeks to create and by the innocence of his character, which is his flaw. His story is familiar to every student of southern fiction. Ashamed of his hill-country origins and his low position in the social structure, he sets out to found a dynasty of Sutpens: he will make his progeny one of the most powerful families of the South.

What Sutpen is really pursuing is a past, though to put the matter this way is to oversimplify the novel. He knows of course that he cannot create a past for himself—that no matter how successful he is in his endeavors to pull himself up by his bootstraps, he cannot escape from the burden of having in the southern sense of the term no history at all. This deprivation he will have to live with, and his determination to do just that is evident in his first encounter with the people of Yoknapatawpha County. He knows that there is nothing he can say about his origins or previous activities that will not do him harm and so he keeps absolutely silent. Later, while he is building the house at Sutpen's Hundred and claiming a plantation from the woods, he displays a kind of controlled desperation by falling back on his physical strength, which he rightly perceives to be his only asset. He fights the largest of his slaves and runs with them through the swamps as if he has deliberately set out to create a legend—a myth that will be acceptable only after generations of genteel family living have established the name of Sutpen and given a romantic patina to the ancient truth.

I said that Sutpen's flaw was his innocence, but the innocence which costs him first the undying enmity of his Haitian wife and finally his life at the hands of Wash Jones also allows him to comprehend with absolute clarity that the design he has in mind—that of establishing a family, a name to be passed from father to son and to accrue respectability in the passing, is the only possible way for him to succeed. Sutpen's character is such—his dimensions so exaggerated, his accomplishments so vast—that he can properly be extrapolated into an image of the South. He is not much different from the Compsons or the Sartorises or the Benbows except that he encompasses in a single lifetime a concatenation of experiences that in most other families would extend through a century and a half. He is not, like Miranda, a literary figure, the writer caught in a historical twilight, seeing for the first time the fallacy within the myth: he never achieves that moment of epiphany that will allow him to comprehend the culture that he exemplifies in all its angularities of good and bad. Sutpen's distortion of values goes beyond anything Amy's family could be capable of, and yet Sutpen's ruthlessness is

a direct product of his proper understanding of the function of family myth.

Sutpen acted in the hope of creating the stuff of a past for
future generations. But the myth must be completed in
remembrance and in an agonizing contemplation of the
ironies of time, and Gail Hightower is a master at this.
Hightower and Joe Christmas and Joanna Burden form a
triumvirate within the larger tapestry of *Light in August*.[10]
Christmas is the quintessential modern man, bereft not
only of family but even of racial identity. He is without the
possibilities or paradigms of myth and therefore without
principles or images to set his life by. He must improvise
day by day until the improvisation itself becomes a way of
getting through life: love turns to hate and then back to
love again; he is white or black according to his whim; he
feels threatened by piety and order. Joanna Burden, on
the other hand, has a past, but not being a southerner, she
declines to make a myth of it. Her grandfather left New
England when he was twelve, sailed the seas, toured the
west, embraced Catholicism and then rejected it. His son,
following in his father's footsteps, was gone from home
sixteen years, returning with a Mexican woman and a
child. This boy was Joanna Burden's half-brother and
along with their grandfather, he was shot by John Sartoris
when he tried to secure the black man's right to vote. For
the Sartorises this encounter at the polling place and its
expiation by Bayard become part of family lore. Joanna
Burden construes the same events only as sacrifices made
on the road to social justice. She lives in the present and

works for the education of the poor until Christmas ends
her life.

So she and Christmas are proper foils for the Reverend
Hightower who is immersed in a legend. Hightower is so
totally committed to the myth, so outrageous in his determination to subordinate every living soul, every contemporary value to the glories of the past that only a writer of
Faulkner's genius could have made him credible. Hightower's behavior is almost completely irrational: he sacrifices not only his own future but his wife's sanity and
finally her life to the constant recollection of his Confederate grandfather, a cavalryman who after a daring and
successful raid was shot while attempting to steal a
chicken. Yet, in spite of his aberration, Hightower
emerges as one of the gentlest and wisest of Faulkner's
people. He counsels Byron Bunch, helps to deliver Lena
Grove's baby, and attempts, at the cost of a broken head, to
save Joe Christmas's life. Hightower is by no means so
imposing or symbolically rich a figure as Sutpen, but he is
first among the keepers of the myth.

Unlike Sutpen's dream, which might have succeeded
had not Bon appeared, or if the war had not come, or had
any of a number of other things not happened, Hightower's worship of his grandfather is hopeless. He wishes
for a vision of the old time—and he is rewarded, mysti-
cally, at the end—but he has been born too late for redemption. For him there can be no cavalry raid, no sound of
bugles and galloping hooves, no shock of steel and smell of
powder. The ancestor worship which replaces his proper
religion is sterile from its inception. Before Hightower is

born, his god is dead. Yet, in his posture of looking stead-
fastly toward the past, he is only an extreme example of a
state of mind that engulfed the South after Appomattox.

We remember Allen Tate's claim that the South was
doomed—whether or not the war had been fought—by
its lack of a proper religion.[11] What we cannot know is
whether the proper religion (Catholicism in Tate's view)
would have saved the South from the dissolution brought
on by the loss of the war and the Reconstruction. In a discussion of gnostic elements in southern society, Lewis P.
Simpson points out that on the eve of the Civil War, the
South looked forward to its own millennium: it posited the
perfectibility of its own society.[12] Mr. Simpson quotes
Robert Barnwell Rhett, who predicted that by the year
2000 a greatly expanded South would have established a
civilization equalled in the history of mankind only by
those of Greece and Rome. Timrod strikes a similar theme
in "Ethnogenesis." Simpson is correct in regarding these
hopes for the future as gnostic in their distorted readings
of human nature and the historical process.

Gnosticism, as Simpson employs the term in his following Eric Voegelin, is "the belief that knowledge available to men can be used to change the very constitution
of being."[13] We are aware that we can build no earthly
paradise so long as the world and mankind remain as they
are, and both mankind and the world resist alteration at
the hands of ordinary mortals who live in ordinary times:
people are perverse; the weather is capricious; nature
continues to follow her inexorable course. But occasion-

ally there comes into being a race of prophets or a messiah who shifts the foundations of reality. After Christ nothing could be the same again, and a besetting temptation of modern generations is to mistake technology and learning for radical accretions of knowledge in the primary sense. In other words, modern man is continually tempted to think that he can modify the terms of human existence and thereby produce the millennium which he desires. He is mistaken because he is not trafficking in essential truth as was Christ, but in secondary realities: at their best in human constructs, at worst in mere appearances. God, human nature, physical and natural law continue the same. But the basic tenet of gnosticism is that the gnostic *does know*, that he shares with the prophets and with Christ a special role in history, and therefore he will neither recant nor desist. Instead he simply postulates a world that he finds amenable to his notions of reality, construes his problems in terms of this postulation, and attempts to enforce hypothetical solutions to misstated problems to the detriment of society and mankind.

Lewis Simpson is able to demonstrate beyond cavil that contemporary man—North and South—is caught up in gnostic madness, and I shall return later to this distressing fact. My immediate concern is with myth and the way in which even a gnostic dream of the future might be moulded, albeit imperfectly, into a mythical structure. Unlike gnosticism myth is *properly* rooted in a clear cold look at conditions as they are. The world is a place of uncertainty and suffering and sorrow. Man's problem is to devise a way by which he can deal with reality by giving his life and the corporate life of the community meaning and hope. According to Mircea Eliade, whose *Cosmos and History* is the basis for the approach I am following, man does this by constructing a myth which will redeem place and time and the agonies inherent in the human condition.[14] This is no place to explain Eliade's theories in detail, but to put them crudely, mundane locations are redeemed by their relationship to holy places on this earth (Golgotha) or to mythical places beyond it (Heaven). Time is redeemed by cycles of repetition and the workings of divine history. Because God rules the universe and has intervened to save us from our sinfulness, we move from the paradise of Eden into which we were born, through the fallen state in which we find ourselves toward the Christian millennium and the next world which we have been promised. Our present state is made habitable because we are conscious of our own guilt and because as a result of the Incarnation we can turn our eyes in hope toward the future.

This is the myth on its highest level, but all other mythical constructs whether actual or false, sacred or profane, have an analogous relationship to it. Under the best of conditions society would arrange itself according to the true and absolute myth as God has revealed it to us, but we live in a different kind of world. Most of our myths are mundane, but nonetheless they are shaped in imitation of the archetype. For example the mythology of the New World is developed in terms of a new discovery of paradise, a new Eden. Eliade points out that Spaniards landing on the soil of America planted a cross in the earth, thus consecrating the territory by a rebirth, a kind of baptism.[15] We know that Faulkner, following the lead of the conquistadores, develops in "The Bear" the idea that Mississippi was the scene of man's second chance to preserve himself from evil. In this brilliant short novel the history of man's fall is played out in microcosm, and redemption is promised, ironically but quite seriously, in the form of a giant snake which appears to Ike McCaslin in the final scene. The directions such a discussion as this can take are too numerous for me even to touch upon. We think immediately of R. W. B. Lewis's theory of the American Adam[16] and Leo Marx's work on the American pastoral.[17] The idea of innocence is inherent to the edenic myth.

But the myths of our time are essentially secular and it is the nature of the secular myth to participate in the gnostic error. As Mr. Simpson makes clear, Rhett and Timrod in postulating their future monuments of human perfection were not essentially different from the boosters who presently run the Atlanta Chamber of Commerce. But in between the dreams of Barnwell Rhett and the erection of the Regency Hyatt, something of great historical and literary significance occurred: the myth by which the South lived assumed its singular delineation and thereby allowed the renascence to take place. Divested of its gnostic character by the events of history, it was at the same time stripped of all future hope: it became entirely a myth of vanished glory. It was a paradigm, a guide, a system to live by; but no idea of restoring the old secular Eden could be entertained.

For over half a century, from the end of the Civil War to the end of the first world war in Europe, the South that has been described many times in literary and historical studies, the South that was prologue to the renascence, endured. Victims of the war and of northern economic oppression, defeated, impoverished, reduced to a reality so far removed from Rhett's vision that the notion of a glorious future South was not only unbelievable but literally undreamable, southerners turned for sustenance to the past. The only comfort was in what had been but could never be again, and because there would be no new golden age, the past would have to be maintained at whatever cost for as long as possible.

How much this southern reverence for the past contributed to the cultural situation that produced the renascence cannot precisely be gauged, but the force was real and powerful. Old moral and metaphysical values survived in the South longer and with greater force than in other sections of the country. Moreover, the southerner's grasp of reality, his experience of desolation which had made him suspicious of the future kept him from a certain kind of naiveté and therefore shielded him from the disillusionment that unbalanced much of Western civilization after World War I. It is instructive to note how little impact the war per se had on southern literature in comparison to the influence it exerted on American letters in general. From *Soldier's Pay* to *A Fable* Faulkner's work that is engendered by the European conflict is distinctly inferior to his usual standard. Donald Davidson and John Crowe Ransom both served on the western front, but neither wrote significant poetry about that war. Given the historical circumstances of the South, it is understandable that the Civil War would capture the southern imagination in a fashion that a more recent war fought on the other side of the ocean would not. I suspect also that the southern mind affected by guilt and disaster, did not suffer the shock of disillusionment that the war with its horrors and political failures brought to others, because southerners were not sufficiently innocent ever to believe in the efficacy of the war and the happy future that abolitionists thought it would guarantee to posterity.

However true all this may be, it seems certain that the culture of the South, based simply on a half myth—a myth of the past, but not of the future—could not continue long into the twentieth century. The twilight of the myth of the past, and therefore the renascence, came in the period between the world wars; by the early fifties the great literary flowering had ended and the moral culture of the South had been weakened to such an extent that it could no longer support artistic endeavor comparable in quality and seriousness to that of the decades immediately preceding. Part of the decline can be accounted for by the decay of Protestant Christianity which had for a while formed a metaphysical base for the larger myth. As a result of change wrought from within and from without—a dilution of the mystery in favor of social programs on one hand, the attacks of science and materialism on the other (which can be seen emblematically in the Scopes trial)—the church in the larger sense became less and less a controlling factor in the lives of men. I would insist that at least from 1865 onward, the influence of the church had been secondary in any event. Heaven and hell still got their due on Sunday; the doctrine of salvation was resurrected at revival time; but the final appeal to moral authority was made more often to the family and to mythical southern heroes such as Lee and Jackson and Forrest than to God. In pursuit of the myth of the past, family piety expanded to enhance the already established concept of community; out of the commonly revered history came a homogeneity of view. There were forces working against the survival of such a culture. As we have seen, it was short on the sacred dimension, the mysterious in the true sense; there was no real way even to make the heroes transcendent, larger than life as are Beowulf or Roland. They remained flesh and blood, worshipped though they were, and therefore, though they resisted mightily, they were ultimately to fall victim to the erosion of time. Of more importance is the fact that their cause, out of which the myth was born, was flawed. To worship the past meant to worship all that the past stood for, and although much of this was good, some of it was bad: the ethic was mundane, imperfect, subject inevitably to change.

By 1946 the renascence was moribund, and its epitaph was quite properly written in political terms. *All the King's Men* is the philosophical swansong, and with a few vagrant exceptions which came later it marks the literal end of the southern renascence. As we are told by Warren, the two characters who come together to form the catastrophic end of the story are fragmented men. Willie Stark is the man of fact, Adam Stanton is the man of idea, and Jack

Burden points out to us that each is drawn to the other by his own incompleteness; each represents a characteristic that the other needs and lacks.[18] Now, almost thirty years later, it seems strange that we should have taken this book so calmly in 1946. To be sure, the literary world celebrated it for the work of genius that it is. The point of view, the plot structure, the thematic design, the language all came under intelligent examination: students and critics argued about the philosophical background and the meaning the novel was meant to convey. The final sentence, to which I should like to address myself presently, became a kind of battle cry for the generation just then entering into a life of professional literary endeavor, all of us, like Miranda, filled with ignorance and hope.

As practitioners of the literary arts, as people, as citizens and southerners, we should have known better. Our own immediate past, the millions of lives sacrificed to nazi and communist ideologies, the further millions, soldiers and civilians alike, killed in armed conflict, the advent of the atomic bomb should have taught us something. All this was only the beginning of a series of dislocations and disasters that was to convince realists of every belief and persuasion that the end of the modern age—that period which began so confidently with the European Renaissance —was and is at hand. It would be inappropriate for me to attempt to make an exhaustive catalogue of our contemporary ailments; and for me to expound the poverty of the present literary situation would be to repeat what I have said elsewhere and to recapitulate with far less grace and learning a thesis Jacques Barzun has developed in *The Use and Abuse of Literature*.[19] All this is germane to Jack Burden's confident assertion that he is going "out of history, into history and the awful responsibility of Time."[20]

Unlike almost every other novel of the southern renascence *All the King's Men* is not rooted in the end of something: the death of the old gods, the old myth, the old dispensation. Instead it is a story of the modern South: a new mythology is developed to replace the old. Willie Stark begins his career as a deadly serious and totally ineffectual candidate for public office. But he learns fast and with a lot of shrewdness and considerable luck he becomes not only the governor but the political dictator of his state. We understand that along with his personal ambition he has a sincere desire to help people, and as the novel progresses he becomes a classic example of the pragmatic mind at work. In his view the end always justifies the means, and the more noble the end the more tawdry the methods that can justifiably be employed to achieve it.

This is a seductive philosophy and it gains a certain credibility from the innate frailty of man. All of us who are called to act in the world are doomed to make mistakes and suffer failures: the nature of the human condition is such that in the pursuit of our most idealistic goals we stumble and must be forgiven again and again. This is why Christ came into the world: to atone for our sins by His own sacrifice and to establish a sacramental system under which erring man might be repeatedly absolved. Still the Christian must attend to the morality of his means as well as to the desirability of his ends, and thus his behavior as well as his philosophical system differ radically from those of Willie Stark. Or to return to the terms that I have thus far been employing, in each case the mythology is different and the myth is the basis on which each man and each system develops its way of dealing with the world.

Cleanth Brooks and other critics have warned us recently of the dangers of trying to make literature do the work of religion.[21] They rightly point out that as our faith in a transcendental reality has withered, we have attempted to impose on poetry and other arts the task of filling the spiritual vacuum that ensues. I see this as a legitimate concern, but the warning comes too late. Already literature has been conscripted to serve the new god of politics—but not politics of the old fashioned sort which sought power for its own sake and for the riches which accrued to the winners. Now political action has become the handmaiden of that same gnosticism. We devise schemes for the perfection of human history, even as our historical situation deteriorates before our eyes. We simply ignore the truth—about mankind and about the human condition. Theories for the construction of a millennium are imposed by political action on the social structure with procrustean ruthlessness. All efforts at dissent are shouted down.

The general effect of such conditions on literature is readily grasped. Gnosticism claims for itself knowledge and power to which it has no title: which is to say that it makes legitimate by its own orders a series of lies. We are told that human nature is ameliorable, that weakness is strength, that license is freedom, that morality is negotiable. I refrain from enumerating specific examples of the sickness to which I am referring here, but my point is that good literature cannot be produced in a society that has become unmoored.[22] The South joined the modern world, assumed the modern world's values, deteriorated as a culture to the point that it could no longer support the production of serious art. But I have another, and in many ways more serious, charge to make.

For the first time in history, so far as I know, a democratic society has forced art into the subservient and dishonest function of pursuing political and social ends. I know how extravagant such an assertion must appear to be and I am equally well aware that as in all such sweeping claims exceptions can be found. Without going on at too-great length, I can support my thesis with reference to a title or two and with a story. A few years ago I had dinner with the author of a novel, then recently published, which deals with the theme of social injustice in the South. In the course of our conversation what I knew anyway became apparent: the author's personal views on the so-called southern question in no way coincided with the orientation of his book. The author simply felt it necessary to compromise with the prevailing intellectual climate in order to get his book published at all. He had written a work at variance with the one he would have written had he been left to his own inspiration.

One may say that such a betrayal of one's vocation is nothing new, that every best seller list is replete with the work of authors who have prostituted themselves. But I think I see in my friend's compromise with principle a weary capitulation to an ambience, a general condition of cultural tyranny that is likely to bring us all to the peculiar kind of resignation that is born of despair. People who would never trim their convictions or vitiate their talents for fame or money collapse under the monolithic imperative of the modern intellectual milieu. All are vanquished by the shibboleths of race, ecology, sexism, and the other nonnegotiable causes of our age.

Even more sad and frightening is the example of the artist so far gone in the usages of the gnostic myth that he has become a part of the mechanism that has robbed him of his freedom. Think, for example, of William Styron. He has all the equipment that a first-rate novelist needs, and he may even be a man of genius, but out of the pressures of our time and whatever perversities work within him, he has wasted himself on the doctrines of existentialism and on his celebrated ideological thrust into the black past. *The Confessions of Nat Turner* is a literary failure in every particular. Its characters—particularly that of Nat—are unconvincing and anachronistic in the worst sense. The plot is manipulated; the message, the propagandistic idea is in total control. Even those whose cause Styron was espousing were not satisfied, nor should they have been.

There are others—Carson McCullers, for instance— who are equally as lost as Styron, but let me return to Warren and the evolution of the myth. In 1914 James Joyce codified a change in the course of our civilization and our literature by legitimatizing the rejections of family and state and church. These were the institutions that had anchored the moral order within which all previous English writers had functioned, and the idea of abandoning them and all that they stood for was the ultimate impulse toward iconoclasm. *A Portrait of the Artist as a Young Man* is an enormously successful, enormously dramatic novel, but by its very success it leaves us adrift in the meaninglessness and absurdity of a faithless world. Warren gives us his own version of *A Portrait* and by this I do not intend to denigrate his originality: he discovers his own material and employs it in his own way with great freshness and skill. But as in Joyce, in *All the King's Men* the old order and the new collide and the old codes of conduct, the old institutions, and the old heroes are destroyed.

With the fading of the homogeneous view born of the lost war, the agrarian orientation, the mistrust of history as process, the sense of the concrete and all the other characteristics typically assigned to southern culture, the myth dies. As we have seen, it was a paradigm of the past only, never of the future, and Jack Burden's entrance into Time and History signaled the beginning of a new dispensation that boded ill for the southern artist and for the culture which had supported him. He found himself not with a tradition still vital and alive, a past still throbbing with the high drama of its heroism and losses, but with a literature about that past. The heroes were gone; the Snopeses and the gnostics had arisen to take their place. Now the new Miranda, whoever and wherever she was, could merely look at novels and stories and poems about the myth that Katherine Anne Porter's Miranda had watched develop and begin to fade while she paused breathless, her emotions, her being precariously balanced between ancient loves and loyalties and the inexorable new day that had begun. For the new Miranda, the new southern writer, there is only time—only the present age and a shelf of great books about an age that she never knew.

TWO

Community

FOR THE NOVELIST THE COMMUNITY PROVIDES—AND IS—
the enveloping action, the milieu in which his characters
pursue their fates. It is the simplest of truisms to point out
that different worlds produce different kinds of literature, that the nineteenth-century English novel is different
in technique and intention from the eighteenth-century
novel because the two societies were different in their
habits and philosophies and manners. We explain modern
literature with all its divisions and uncertainties in terms of
the age in which we live, and looking back over the history
of literature insofar as we can trace it, we can see that some
ages were better for creative activity than others. My concern here is not with the mysterious chemistry that works
between a writer and his society or with what historical
situations are most conducive to the creation of literary
art. Instead I want to address myself to the use the writer
makes of the society he writes about or, more specifically,
to the function of community in the novels of the southern
renascence.

Consider, for example, *The Long Night* by Andrew Lytle.
In this novel, published in 1936 and never, I think, given
the attention it deserves, Lytle exploits most of the aspects
of southern community that engage the major figures of

the renascence such as Faulkner and Welty and Tate. First, there is the family which is the basic organization on which community is built. The McIvors, seeking greener pastures, leave their more settled environment near the coast and move, not long before the Civil War, into the less ordered world of rural Alabama. Here the elder McIvor is murdered by members of a criminal syndicate which has gained control of the community, and the McIvor clan in all its collateral dimensions is called together to plan its assault on the prevailing forces of evil and its revenge on those who killed one of their own.

The scene is typical of the best effects that Andrew Lytle can achieve, and there is nothing quite like it in any other southern novel. In all his work Lytle sees the family as image, and he strives to make it function as social force and as metaphysical reality. People gathered together under one roof—old and young, male and female, rich and poor, refined or crass according to their natures and circumstances—exhibit because of their common blood, itself based on the sacrament of marriage, a unity neither arbitrary nor subject to personal taste or the vicissitudes of history. Whatever individuals may ultimately feel for each other, whatever disputes may rend them, family relationships are inviolable: Cain and Abel remain brothers; cousins are cousins whether they love each other or not. Early communities—for instance, the tribes of Israel—were extensions of the family. And the perfect community, the City of God, never to be achieved under a mundane dispensation, is a family bound together under the fatherhood of a Creator.

But in the reality of the human situation, family is not

all. There is also the larger and more powerful but arbitrary construct of government. It exercises authority, but it is subject to change; it commands the loyalty of some of its citizens and the contempt of others. Again in a perfect world the services that it requires of its people would be always identical with the best interests of families and of individuals. But only under circumstances of extreme disaster, war or natural calamity, are the demands of government and the legitimate desires of individuals likely to be coterminous. Normally community is the product of a compromise between the order imposed by the political and social organization and the freedom of each man to go his own way. Literature, particularly the novel, concerned as it is with the texture of life, discovers the ground for much of its drama in the tension that exists between the realms of public and private concern, the calls of public and private duty. Or, as in the example of *Hamlet*, the assault on the probity of government and on the felicity of the family is combined in one antagonist or action. Such is the case at the beginning of *The Long Night*.

When the meeting of the large family connection has been played to its conclusion—and it is fraught with contention and even disgust on the parts of some who have come from far away—Pleasant McIvor has assumed the role of avenger. He will scourge those persons who have been involved in the murder of his father, and in doing this he will cleanse the community at large, which suffers under the domination of the criminal gang. The story, as everyone who has read the novel knows, is brilliantly executed. "Like all good tales," as Warren has observed, "it has

its own life and will, and works its will on us."[1] Lytle is
skillful at developing suspense and describing action, and
while Pleasant is stalking his victims, Lytle is busy bringing
them to life, showing their vices and virtues and their
relationships with each other and with the people around
them so that a sense of community, flawed but not totally
dominated by evil, begins to emerge. Those who are about
to die eat, sleep, love, hope, and sustain each other in their
common fear and need.

An ambiguity develops which adds richness to the novel's fabric but clouds its motivation: here as is frequently
the case, the usages and dispositions of a democratic society
complicate the writer's task. There is no king in Alabama
to function in the novel as ruler in fact and as symbol of the
corrupted authority of government. Vengeance cannot be
accomplished and public order reestablished by the single
act of killing the leader of the criminal band. A little more
than halfway through *The Long Night* McIvor has his confrontation with his adversary. The two men face each
other in a darkened room in what ought to be the climactic
and purifying moment of the novel. But nothing happens.
You cannot kill me, Tyson Lovell tells McIvor, because to
get the satisfaction you desire you must kill all the rest of
my followers first. And this will be impossible because the
Civil War has begun.[2] Lovell's old group will be dispersed
among the Confederate divisions where its members will
be out of Pleasant's reach.

There is, if I may extend the comparison to Shakespeare, an obvious similarity between Hamlet's refusal to
kill Claudius while he is at his prayers and Pleasant's desire

to leave the murder of Lovell as the final act in his scenario
of revenge. But the differences in the two situations are
deeply significant. Hamlet in his reluctance to kill a pray-
ing enemy clearly oversteps the bounds of his commission:
his task is to set right the wrongs of the world, but not to
help select the population of heaven. He misunderstands
his mortality and his mission as God's minister. McIvor's
rejection of his chance to murder Lovell is sheer self-
indulgence. For the form of the thing and for his own
personal satisfaction, he will wait. And because he makes
this choice, the novel seems to me to trail off badly in its
closing third. The private action of the novel is also over-
whelmed by the public action of the war.

Yet it is the last part of the novel that confronts directly
the discrepancy between public and private duty. Once he
is in the Confederate army, McIvor continues to kill those
men, now themselves soldiers, who were in any way con-
nected with the death of his father. But the community,
which was once the small neighborhood around the
McIvor farm in Alabama, has grown under the exigencies
of war to include the entire Confederacy. The quest for
personal vengeance, which once could be viewed as an
effort to purify the community, has now become inimical
to the public good. The army and therefore the nation are
endangered by McIvor's private vendetta and when this
fact becomes clear to him, he deserts the army, abandons
forever his plans for revenge, and retires to the hills.
Thus, in its way, the novel comes full circle. Public and
private duty which coincide in action at the beginning of
the narrative, draw apart as historical circumstances shift

the base of community, then come together once more in the rejection of action at the novel's end.

As I have indicated, the novel is not totally satisfactory, and I think the reason is that community cannot be defined or encompassed by the war per se. The holocaust calls too much attention to itself: its noises are too shrill, its heroism too stark, its suffering too acute; and above all, the issues of battle are too simple. Yet nothing has shaped southern history and therefore southern community as extensively as the fact of the war, and consequently the novelist must make some use of it. One solution is to write around it, to keep it large in the consciousness of the reader, but to work short of the actualities of combat, to remain at the periphery of hostilities in time and space.

Consider Allen Tate's *The Fathers*.[3] This novel, published two years after *The Long Night*, presents in its opening chapter one of the most famous and successful of all renditions of southern community. The scene is Pleasant Hill, plantation home of the Buchans; the time is 1860; the old Virginia family have gathered for the burial of Mrs. Buchan, mother of Lacy, the narrator of the book. Lacy's mind wanders from present to past, backward and forward over time, and with the pattern of his observations and recollections the image of community and the threats to its continued existence join in developing the theme and conflict of the novel. Major Buchan, Lacy's father, is one of the old breed and perhaps the last of his kind. He sees life as totally ordered and totally integrated, and therefore he makes no distinctions between society and government, between the individual and the state and even the nation in which he lives. All levels of experience, all ramifications of human affairs are held together by memory—a respect for the past and the customs and manners which have been authenticated by tradition. In the larger organization of Major Buchan's world, everyone has a place. The plantation is ruled by the master and the mistress, duties and obligations divided between them according to what is suitable to the male or female talent: the affairs of the house for the lady, business and the fields for the man. Beneath the parents are the children, beneath the children are the servants, but within and parallel to these larger categories are minor hierarchies of rank and privilege, universally recognized and never to be transgressed. All this is very familiar to anyone who has even a passing acquaintance with the social structure of the old South. Equally familiar is the code according to which the community organization is maintained and by which its dispensations are enforced.

The most venerable of all southern stories, the grand theme that in one way or another informs so much of southern fiction is the struggle between those southerners who embrace the concept of community and abide by the code and those who are indifferent to the tradition. Critics of *The Fathers* have rightly made much of the fact that Major Buchan is frustrated in his dealings with George Posey because Posey is, among other things, a modern man.[4] Accosted by Major Buchan in the office at Pleasant Hill, Posey will not be shaken by the words the major speaks to him—"I tell you, sir, that we do not deserve your kindness"[5]—or see the rebuke in Major Buchan's continuing to wear his hat. And when the major has used the old forms in all their nuances, he is done. If Posey appears dressed as a gentleman, bearing the name and occupying the place of a gentleman, and yet refuses to conduct himself according to the code of a gentleman, then Major Buchan is helpless against him. For to fight Posey on his own terms is to become like him, which means the end of community and the abandonment of the code.

The difference between Posey and Major Buchan is drawn precisely at the funeral of Mrs. Buchan. The major's good manners in the midst of his grief are at once a manifestation of and a foundation for southern community. His friends and his neighbors, his immediate society, are in his house, and regardless of what he feels personally, he is obliged by the rules under which he lives to treat them with cordiality and to be mindful of their comfort. Real manners are never merely superficial. Major Buchan's mode of behavior is indicative of an accommodation that he and those who share his views and habits have made with death. It is a part of life, and therefore life does not stop for it, nor does mortal flesh quail before the grim finality. The continued functioning of the community makes bearable to the individual the suffering that must be borne.

Posey, a city man and therefore one bereft of a sense of life's totality, cannot face the obsequies of his mother-in-law. He is a private being who doubtless means well, but his loyalties cannot be engaged on the level of community. It is worth noting—and I have discussed the matter at some length elsewhere[6]—that Posey's only source of

strength is his religious background: the Roman Catholicism that Mr. Tate saw as the proper religion for the Old
South. But Posey is not a pious man and as a consequence
he drifts through life in the modern fashion, a victim of
situation ethics, a moral and spiritual *franc tireur*. Posey's
character, done in depth and complexity, is the finest
accomplishment in Tate's generally impressive book. In
his posture as antagonist to Major Buchan and all that the
major stands for, Posey develops a frightening but seductive strength.

Early in the novel Tate gives us a scene that in less
skillful hands would degenerate into parody. The young
gentlemen of the neighborhood—the flower of the
community—mask themselves in the fashion of medieval
knights and before a gallery of beribboned ladies, they
ride at the ring. Posey's presence gives this sequence a
ballast of reality. The horse he mounts has been bought
with proceeds from the sale of his mulatto half brother.
And having won the tournament, he immediately violates
established community usage by refusing a duel and then
striking his adversary with his fist. Something in this
pattern of behavior, the practical thrust undeterred by
romantic trappings, enflames Susan's affections. She an-
nounces that she will marry Posey before she knows
whether Posey has killed John Langdon or even whether
there has been a duel in the proper sense.

Yet it would be wrong to claim that Posey acts merely to
suit himself. Instead, all his motives derive out of his isolation from society and community. The personal quality of
his vision cannot transcend itself. The effect is ambivalent.
Unencumbered by a devotion to his own people, he is not

tempted to believe in the myth of southern invincibility: he knows that logistics will win the war. Voted out of a commission by the company he has paid to equip, he feels neither anger nor disgrace because he is indifferent to the opinion of his neighbors. He takes up gun-running for the Confederacy and turns a profit for himself. But the same detachment from traditional attitudes and behavior makes a shambles of his personal life.

His neglect of Susan after they are married is a product not of carelessness for her feelings but of Posey's inability to comprehend the most rudimentary demands of human intercourse. Since he is himself totally self-sufficient, he expects her to thrive in his house in Georgetown where disorder reigns among the servants and the adults come and go according to no system and keep their thoughts to themselves. Susan's outrage turns to anger, her anger to hatred; and she takes her revenge by inducing the sordid events that she hopes will lead young Jane, Posey's sister, to a convent and Yellow Jim, Posey's half-brother, to his death. But Susan's brother Semmes also dies because even Susan is unable to fathom the absolutely personal quality of Posey's moral life.

Posey is an anachronism, a prophetic figure not only in advance of the time of the novel but ahead of the year in which the book appeared. He will come upon the American scene in the decades that follow World War II—the completely private citizen, at odds with his government and ignorant of the very existence of community: he loves no place or people; he has no loyalty save to himself. Thus it is proper that he should exit during the last scene of *The Fathers*, an enigmatic figure riding away to a destination that is everywhere and in the future and therefore must, within the novel, remain undefined. "I love him more than I love any man,"[7] says Lacy, who remains to fight at First Manassas. And so have we loved him after more than a hundred years.

Posey's defects must not be allowed to blind us to the imperfections of community in the South. In spite of his virtues Major Buchan has no business or agricultural acumen, and his insistence on farming according to tradition as well as behaving by the old standards has brought Pleasant Hill to the verge of ruin before the war begins. The plantation is saved by Posey who sells slaves Major Buchan intends to free, and the major's innocence in matters of commerce extends to his judgment of the political realities which rise to threaten the modes by which he lives. On the eve of the war Major Buchan inserts into his morning devotions a prayer to be used when calamity threatens the family, thus reasserting an identity of public and private loyalty, public and private duty which no longer obtains. He disowns his son who joins the Confederate army, but later chooses death rather than submit to the crass Union soldiers who come to burn his home. Major Buchan's self destruction is perhaps intended to be an act of deep significance, but I shall not press this interpretation. It is sufficient to say that his inability or refusal to perceive the historical mutations of southern community cost him his life.

Allen Tate, seeing more clearly than anyone else except for his friend and master T. S. Eliot the fragmentations of contemporary civilization, gives us in *The Fathers* an image of what that forlorn figure at the cemetery gate feels and endures in "Ode to the Confederate Dead." [8] Faulkner's fictional range, though less stark, was broader; and he shows how the concept of community functioned in the South during and immediately after the Civil War. As we see in *The Unvanquished*, [9] when the strong go forth to conquer or to die, their duties, including that of maintaining the social order, devolve upon the weak. The book, which is unified more by theme than by plot, opens on a note of deceptive simplicity: a boyish prank which results in the death of a horse and an amusing confrontation between a Yankee colonel and Bayard Sartoris's grandmother, Rosa Millard. But beneath the light tonality of the narrative surface the major conflict of the book is being prepared. Granny is forced to lie to the colonel, which seems harmless enough, since the colonel knows that she is lying; but in this comic moment the basic moral disintegration which accompanies community disorientation has begun.

Andrew Lytle, in a brilliant essay on *The Unvanquished*, [10] illuminates Faulkner's use of physical imagery to convey the dissolution of the social fabric. Granny and the two boys move along roads that are either made dangerous by skirmishing soldiers or impassable by thousands of ex-slaves who have been turned loose upon the world. The Negroes go they know not where, raising clouds of dust, moaning in their hunger and weariness and dropping out along the way to die. Granny's efforts to restore order are futile against the human tide from which all individual conscience and responsibility have vanished. The shells of burned houses, the destroyed railroads and bridges reenforce the sense of cultural dismemberment, the failure of community under the stress of war.

Granny will not abandon those things on which her civilization, if it is ever to be restored, must rest. She carries rose cuttings on her various peregrinations, and with Ringo's help she reclaims her stolen silver and by a concatenation of errors finds herself with a great deal more silver and a great many more mules than she originally lost. I do not want to insist on the symbolic value of roses and silver. For Faulkner they may have been only realistic details—the surface truth that deepens in meaning because it is the truth. But they are there along with the umbrella which Mr. Lytle sees as a staff of office, effectual only for the respect it engendered in the old world where social order reigned.[11]

What begins for Granny as a quest for private justice evolves into an effort to reestablish the community which has been destroyed by war. Having got back her own mules, she continues to steal animals from the Federal army in order to furnish stock to the poor and starving people who have no means with which to farm. The careful records that she keeps of her transactions are indicative of her desire to reorganize an amorphous group of suffering individuals into an interdependent body, and at this stage of her career her private desire and her public duty coincide. But once she turns away from her efforts to rebuild the community, she is doomed by her wish for strictly personal gain. Attempting to deal with the horse thief Grumby in the hope of making money for her son-in-law John Sartoris who must rebuild his life now that the war is ending, she meets her death. Later in the novel Sartoris moves to his own end along a similar path. Having fought in the war and come home to the chaos of Reconstruction, he employs the derringer he carries up his sleeve to reimpose the antebellum status quo. Two carpetbaggers are killed, illiterate black candidates are removed from political office, the names of blacks, most of them signed with X's, are expunged from the voter rolls. Thus a system of social order, a community much like the one which operated before the Federal invasion is reestablished. But Sartoris cannot stop killing and he cannot adjust himself to the changes that accrue with time. He attempts to build a railroad, but as we know from the example of George Posey in *The Fathers*, technology and progress complicate the distinction of public duty and move the individual more and more toward the isolation of a private view. Sartoris cannot eschew the violence by which he has lived most of his life, but with human actions becoming more complicated and motivations more difficult to discern, he can no longer justify to himself a continuation of bloodshed. So, morally confused by the altered circumstances of civil existence, he chooses to die under the community code to which he was born and which he helped to sustain.

I find the end of *The Unvanquished* a noble but unsatisfactory effort to solve a problem that cannot be solved. In the section entitled "An Odor of Verbena" Faulkner attempts to rectify by a single heroic act of synthesis the

Christian ethos with the demands of community in the South. If we really believe the Bible, Bayard (now grown) admonishes himself, then we have to believe that God meant for us not to kill each other, and Bayard is therefore called upon to avenge the death of his father without sacrificing another life.[12] As all who have read the novel will remember, Bayard goes unarmed to the office of his father's adversary Redmond, allows himself to be shot at and by sheer moral force and a display of incredible bravery forces Redmond to put down his own gun and to leave town.

We know from history and from literature that the solution is not so easy. I do not quite believe the scene between Bayard and Redmond, even on an individual level; and I certainly cannot see it as a pattern for action, an adumbration of a better day that is to come. Faulkner himself in *Light in August, Intruder in the Dust, Sanctuary* and other fictions, all of which take place later in time than *The Unvanquished*, shows us the bad side of community action, the sense of public duty set in motion with or without provocation, which exacts penalties that may or may not be just. In the South, once the Civil War has ended, the public dimension ceases to be discovered in the political organization and is found rather in a paragovernmental sense of the society which asserts itself in the worst as well as the best of ways. The same community which lynches Joe Christmas and ostracizes Gail Hightower[13] allows Miss Emily Grierson to go without paying her taxes or being harassed about the dreadful odor that for a while poisons the air around her house.[14] The old ladies in *The Unvanquished* assert a strength that no mere government could muster when they force John Sartoris and Drusilla to marry in deference to the purity of womanhood and the sanctity of the home. But once the war is over there are no more Major Buchans. No one any longer prays for the family when the national or even the local government is threatened. The community is a group of believers operating under the myth and according to the usages of the past.

The period in the development of southern community which produced the renascence is also the time in which some of the very best southern fiction is set. Eudora Welty's *The Golden Apples*[15] is built in much the same way and begins in the same fashion as *The Unvanquished*, though it is a denser and more complicated novel. In the opening chapter Katie Rainey tells the story of Snowdie MacLain whose husband King spends most of his time away from home. The particular scene depicts one of King MacLain's few defeats: he is driven from his own front porch by his twin sons who are emboldened by their halloween masks and who do not recognize their own father. The situation is comic and, as we come to see, ironic in the justice of its outcome, but of more importance it introduces the idea of family, here violated, which is the basis for community. Snowdie without her husband is a woman bereft: she exists outside the mainstream of the social organization in Morgana. All of this is prelude to the agonies of Miss Eckhart and of the orphans at Moon Lake and of the MacLain twins once they are grown and of the chief of the wanderers, Virgie Rainey.

Miss Eckhart is the main character in "June Recital,"[16]

which is certainly one of the very best sequences in Miss Welty's distinguished canon. Miss Eckhart is German, as her name implies, though perhaps not born abroad, and strange in her accent and her turn of phrase; her ancestry is unknown beyond the old mother she brings with her, and she is a member of a church that is not even represented in Morgana. It is one of the great technical strengths of the book that we see Miss Eckhart always at a kind of psychological distance and always through the eyes of others. She gives piano lessons to the children of Morgana; and her recitals, which coincide with the end of school, mark the unofficial start of summer. She has two loves, both of which remain unfulfilled partly as a result of fate, partly because of her isolation and the need the community feels to exclude her.

First there is Mr. Sissum, a clerk at the shoe store whom Miss Welty brings to life with characteristic skill in a single paragraph. Mr. Sissum is given to gentle sarcasm and much good humor: he invites large ladies to sit in the childrens' chairs and treats shoes "as though they were something predestined."[17] But he leaves off jokes in his kind and solicitous treatment of Miss Eckhart. His courtship with Miss Eckhart is almost nonexistent, a relationship so slight that only Miss Welty could have given it the piquancy and meaning that it generates. Displaying an old maid's incompetence at romance, Miss Eckhart buys several pairs of shoes at a time, though the shoe store is the only place where she can advance her acquaintance with Mr. Sissum. Because she is a Lutheran, they cannot meet at church, and on holidays he plays the cello with the orchestra in the park while she sits on the grass and listens. In the evenings he furnishes music at the movie theater which is owned by his brother. Then he is drowned in a fishing accident, and Miss Eckhart makes such an open display of her grief that some of the women in town withdraw their daughters from her tutelage.

The other object of Miss Eckhart's affection is Virgie Rainey. Virgie is vastly talented, and Miss Eckhart is determined that she should leave Morgana, pursue advanced study, and make her name in the world. But for the citizens of Morgana, Morgana is the world, and Virgie Rainey is simply one of the Raineys who peddle milk and vegetables on the streets and ice cream at political gatherings. It is all well and good that Virgie can conquer difficult pieces and play "Für Elise" at the June recital, but the cheap ribbon of her sash fades on her dress and her mother wears the same hat year after year and the same unrestrained smile for her daughter's accomplishments. Her genius notwithstanding, Virgie remains at the periphery of the community and the Presbyterian music scholarship is awarded to Cassie Morrison. Finally Miss Eckhart is assaulted by a crazy Negro man and soon after that the war with Germany begins and she loses her remaining students.

All of this, as readers of *The Golden Apples* know, takes place before the present action of "June Recital." At the opening of the chapter Loch Morrison, sick with malaria and bored beyond endurance by his summer incarceration, watches the house next door through his telescope. The effect is spatial, as if one were observing the action on a stage: Virgie Rainey on a bed with a sailor upstairs, and below Miss Eckhart festooning the living room with newspapers. Miss Eckhart is old now and lives in the county asylum. She is not quite sane as her behavior demonstrates, but this parodic reenactment of the best part of her past conveys the bitter disappointments that life has dealt her. In other Junes the room was gay with colored streamers. Now she hangs strips of newsprint from the chandelier, and except for her own incompetence and the appearance of the sheriff who happens by she would burn the house down.

Virgie, flushed from her tryst with the sailor by the smoke and the noise, runs a gauntlet of Morgana ladies returning from a session of Rook, passing Miss Eckhart with no word of greeting or even nod of the head. The two outcasts go their own way: Miss Eckhart back to her institutional bed, Virgie to the movie house where she has replaced Mr. Sissum in furnishing an accompaniment to the silent pictures. And the community, represented by the ladies on their way home from the party, remains what it is, its stability, for the time being at least, inviolate. "I see you, Virgie Rainey," Miss Billie Texas Spights declares,[18] thus reaffirming the power of society as distinguished from the mere force of law and civil authority which are represented by the comic sheriff and his fumbling deputy. Those who deviate from the community norm are punished by general ridicule and isolation.

The same theme is probed in "Moon Lake,"[19] but with the addition of existential undertones and the introduction of death as the ultimate measure of our common humanity. At the camp on Moon Lake the Morgana girls have been joined by a group from the orphanage. The leader of the orphans is a tough character with a dirty neck who seems, on first meeting, totally self-sufficient. Unlike the town girls, who are members of the community and therefore know who they are, Easter has named herself— she has mispronounced Esther—and if she was ever told who her father is, she has forgotten. Jenny Love Stark and Nina Carmichael who spend an afternoon with Easter are at first intimidated and angered by her. They are helpless against her superficial talents, her ability to play mumblety-peg and to drink from a stream without a cup and to fend off their girlish taunts with cool indifference. But anger turns to unbearable pity when they learn that she was delivered to the orphanage by her own mother as soon as she was old enough to walk. Jenny Love and Nina can respond to this outrage only by hitting each other.

On another afternoon, lying on her cot while the girls around her are sleeping, Nina wonders what it would be like to be Easter. This is the old question of identity made fresh by Miss Welty's casting it in terms of the vast social difference that exists between those who are securely a part of the Morgana world and those who have no identity and in a way no existence. Among other things Nina wants to be sure that Easter exists, for the question of being, of life in the pure sense, is not a matter for discussion within the assured delineations of community. That Nina should lie awake and try to fathom the depths of Easter's existential center is evidence that some of the foundations and assumptions of community are being called into question.

Near the end of this part of the novel Easter falls into the lake and almost drowns. She is rescued and revived by Loch Morrison, who never wanted to be at a girls' camp in the first place, and the process of artificial respiration is long and arduous. Miss Lizzie Stark arrives with watermelons for the campers and is disgraced to see Easter face down on the picnic table and Loch astride her. The scene has that extraordinary richness that is the hallmark of Miss Welty's best work. The presence of death—for all think that Easter has truly drowned—brings the town girls close to Easter in a way that even Nina Carmichael finds uncomfortable. And against this instance of mankind's common doom the conventional usages of community are utterly frivolous. Miss Lizzie's cry of outrage that Loch should be on top of the prostrate girl is, in reality, her helpless cry against fate, the noise she makes in receiving this hint that the customs of social probity will not save her.

The community in *The Golden Apples*, based as it is on the myth and habits of the past, begins to disintegrate not so much under the assaults of progress as under the existential and metaphysical demands of the human soul. With the passing of time, Morgana changes: people grow old and die; children grow up and marry. But the landscape remains largely the same, and even at the end, manners and social procedures show little alteration. When, as the action draws to a close, Miss Katie Rainey dies, neighbors come in to lay out her body and the members of the community bring food and flowers and stay to sit with the corpse and to visit with each other. The title of this section is "The Wanderers,"[20] and wanderers have become more numerous in Morgana since King MacLain set his early example. MacLain is still alive, almost a hundred his grandchildren say, and age has forced a mutation in his concupiscence. His passion now is for food—country ham, hot coffee. But he does not repudiate or regret his past: he boasts of the trips that once he was able to make, thus challenging death with the life that he has posited against extinction.

There are others who deviate from community values. The MacLain twins have had their adventures, one in California where a long sequence of the novel takes place, the other through a stormy marriage and a sad illicit love affair in Morgana. But the real wanderers are the true outsiders, those whom the community would never fully accept: Miss Eckhart and Virgie Rainey. The strength and the weakness of community meet at the obsequies of Katie Rainey. One of the proofs of Miss Welty's great genius is her ability to handle large groups of people. She gives us a tableau of the Morgana world at large, the entire company on stage before the very final pages of the book are turned over to Virgie's healing ruminations. Old men talk quietly; women move from dining room to kitchen; young wives complain; preachers proselyte; children play in the yard without ever quite breaching the general decorum. This is community at its best, and to know its value, we need simply to bring to mind our own funerary practices—the mortuary, the mausoleum, the crematoreum.

Even at its best, community, short of the City of God, cannot be entirely truthful. It is important to the survival of social structures that relationships take precedence over human impulse. Virgie's mother has been one of the burdens of Virgie's life, a source not of joy but of deprivation. In the afternoon, following her full day's work, Virgie has come home to milk her mother's cows and to endure her mother's harassment. We are led to believe that she has never married because of her mother. Friends offer their condolences by telling Virgie that she does not know what she has lost. But Virgie knows all too well. "I'll sell the cows to the first white man I meet on the road,"[21] she says to herself. She gives her mother's china and whatever else they might want to the Negroes. Then she walks alone in the rain, remembering Miss Eckhart.

It is significant, I think, that the novel ends on a note of reconciliation between the two outsiders. Miss Eckhart is, of course, long dead by now, but Virgie at last sees the affection that existed between them. And the discovery does not come too late: it is not obliterated by the passage of time or by tardy discovery. Both Virgie and Miss Eckhart have been thwarted by the community, penalized by their helpless or deliberate deviation from its imperatives, but each of them has endured life, which is a kind of victory. Virgie remembers the picture of Perseus holding the head of Medusa that once hung on Miss Eckhart's wall.[22] Perseus had avoided being turned to stone by approaching the enchantress obliquely: he had worked from her reflection in his polished shield, which is to say, by a kind of indirection.

This is all, and it is enough. For Virgie there is no rebellion, no confrontation with the society that has been her support at times, but more often her persecutor. She can accept her freedom with a gratitude untainted by bitterness. She can find some comfort in the remembrance of love. She can even take a kind of ironic joy in the spiritual kinship she feels with the old black woman who pauses beside her. But Virgie's posture in the very last scene of the book, her lonely vigil in the rain, is an image of that perilous and pregnant moment in the development of southern culture to which I have referred earlier: the beginning of the end of community, the start and later the finish of the renascence. Her silence in which the claims of public and private loyalties are buried is a harbinger of the tension that accompanies the dissolution of community and of the chaos that ultimately will ensue.

THREE

Rainbow's End

IN MY FIRST TWO LECTURES I HAVE ATTEMPTED TO DESCRIBE the death of myth and the decay of community in the South; and I am aware that in the process I have slighted and perhaps even begged the overwhelming question. Even if one grant that the mythic vision and the sense of community have deteriorated, does this mean necessarily that the renascence has ended? Could it not be, as such critics as Louis Rubin and Lewis Simpson have held in this series, that the renascence has entered a new phase, different from the old, but lively and productive, achieving successes almost as grand as those of the renascence at its richest? I see no way to answer this question except to compare the literature of the here and now with that of the twenties and thirties and early forties. On other occasions, I have suggested that Faulkner's best work was finished with the publication of *Go Down, Moses* in 1942, that Warren's best novel is *All the King's Men*, that Katherine Anne Porter's *Ship of Fools* is a disappointment.[1] These judgments are probably shared by the majority of responsible critical opinion, but conclusions based on the judgments vary. Some writers do their best work when they are young, some when they are older. It can be argued that the social and philosophical alterations which afflicted southern society after World War II were incidental; that Faulkner's major phase was over in any event, and that to link the two phenomena together is to commit a variation of the *post hoc* fallacy. My response to this is that the cumulative evidence is too great to be ignored. The work of every southern writer who came to prominence between the great wars diminishes in quality in the fifties and sixties and early seventies.

Obviously, the difficulty is not a loss of technical competence. Writers are not athletes whose legs might give out at the beginning of a season or whose performance suffers once they start wearing spectacles. Through their working lives, artists retain their skills and some of them save the best for last. Shakespeare's *A Winter's Tale* and *The Tempest* are universally admired: *Don Quixote* is the work of an old man writing at the height of his power, as is Thomas Mann's *Doctor Faustus*. We do know, however, that literary technique, the measurable qualities of a work, such as rime and meter and imagery in poetry and structure and scene and characterization in fiction are adjuncts of artistic vision. When the writer is wrong about life, his work turns sour. When he has nothing to say, his technical abilities accommodate themselves to his situation. When his society becomes fragmented, the uncertainty of the writer's moral vision is reflected in every aspect of his artistic creation. The most recent work of Eudora Welty is a case in point.

I have already declared my admiration for Miss Welty's fiction, and she better than anyone else exemplifies the old guard significantly at work in the new setting. It is important to note, I think, that the brilliant novel *Losing Battles* is a long look backward. The action is very carefully circumscribed in terms of both time and place; it is set in the middle 1930s and consequently none of the agonies of our own situation in history are allowed to intrude. But *The Optimist's Daughter* is contemporary and though it is much shorter and less complex, the funeral scene around which the book is organized reminds us of the last triumphant segment of *The Golden Apples*. In *The Optimist's Daughter* Morgana is replaced by Mount Salus, but the physical surroundings make little difference: the alteration is seen in the weakening community, the clouding of individual relationships, the diminution of the characters and their loss of a sense of self.

The modern question of individual identity is not new to Miss Welty's work. In my discussion of *The Golden Apples* I referred to Easter who, being an orphan, has no place in the community and no past. She does not know who she is or where she has come from or what role she is meant to fill in the future. Laurel McKelva, who is the optimist's daughter, is a more sophisticated and modernized exemplar of the human being adrift in the world and uncertain of her own destinations. Indeed I take the theme of *The Optimist's Daughter* to be the search for human integration into life itself, the continuum of time and the relationship of individuals to each other in the past as well as in the present.

Laurel McKelva is no Virgie Rainey, though we cannot escape observing that she is what Virgie might have been under better circumstances. Laurel's talent is for art, and having been raised in comfortable, if not luxurious, conditions, she has studied design in Chicago. Widowed since shortly after her marriage, she lives and works there. She is a wanderer, and when she comes home for her father's sickness and death and funeral, she must try to fathom the excesses of both of her parents which have helped to shape her life in ways that she cannot fully know and which have left their scars upon her. The book is filled with life, as Miss Welty's work always is, but at crucial moments, at turns in the story where we look for revelations, we find not so much ambiguity as uncertainty.

Before his death Judge McKelva has married a vulgar girl from Texas whose family surprise her by coming to the judge's funeral. Uncomplicated as they are, Fay's mother and brother and sister and nieces and nephews comprise some of the best characterizations in the novel. From the beginning of her career Miss Welty has done ill-bred people with unrelenting accuracy, and Fay's relatives have a genius for barbarism based on a kind of pure and undisguised selfishness: they share an incredible gift for doing and saying the wrong thing. But the quality of shock they bring to the novel is not based merely on bad manners or flawed human nature. In the last segment of *The Golden Apples* we see essentially the same kind of people, but their worst qualities and the harshness of their conduct are meliorated by their legitimate place and function within the community. Rich or poor, gifted or otherwise, they know and respect each other, and because they value their reputations they conduct themselves better than might otherwise be the case. It is true that the

Chisolms in *The Optimist's Daughter* come from another state, but this is a matter of emphasis I think, meant to point up but not to account for their separateness. In the modern South as in the world at large, we all imitate George Posey by moving toward the shelter of our own private judgments. Otherwise why would Laurel have exiled herself from the place and the past which, as she knows, harbor the roots of her being?

As the novelist skillfully demonstrates, one of the difficulties of our modern predicament is to recover memory in its original dimensions. Major Bullock stands by the coffin and spins heroic yarns about his dead friend, but what he says has no foundation in reality. Laurel protests, but the fantasizing continues. We are left to wonder not what is truth: we can find that; we can discover the facts, the dates, the actions. It is the quality of life and of the past, the meanings of existence that elude us. We look in vain for the heroic action around which to organize the past and by which to measure the present. In *The Fathers* the ghost of the old grandfather says to Lacy Buchan, "My son, in my day we were never alone,"[2] and Virgie Rainey, misused and eager to escape though she may be, can still find the meaning of the past by her reconciliation with Miss Eckhart at the end of *The Golden Apples*. In *The Optimist's Daughter* Laurel achieves no more than an uneasy peace with life and time before she leaves Mount Salus forever, we suppose, and goes back to Chicago.

With her usual virtuosity Miss Welty balances against each other the three women who share the love of Judge McKelva: Laurel and Fay and Becky, his first wife who is dead before the novel opens. Becky, as Laurel reconstructs her from remembered experience and notebooks and old letters, is a woman of great strength and great fidelity to old affections. At age fifteen she went, in the depths of winter, alone down the river on a raft with her sick father; and she returned with his body after his death in Baltimore. She could do this, we are told, because she knew herself and her capacity, because she was confident in her understanding of all the aspects of the existence to which she was born: her grandmother and her mother and her six devoted brothers, the house high on a mountain top, the animals and woods and wild strawberries. Home to her was always West Virginia, not Mount Salus, and through the long days of her final illness, memories of that home caused her to rail against her husband and daughter and the efforts they made to show their devotion to her and to ease her pain. We see her clearly for what she represents—an almost Aristotelian figure in her excess of virtue; her proper but extreme love of her past vitiates her later attachments.

Fay—without past or present, ashamed of her family, outraged that the judge should have sickened and died, conscious only of her own convenience and pleasure—is the absolute opposite of Becky. Judge McKelva, Laurel tells us, loved his first wife too much and his second too little, and her diagnosis is authenticated by the events of the story. Having lived through the agony of Becky's death, he will not duplicate it by allowing himself to linger. And with all of this, as with her own widowhood, Laurel must make an accommodation. It is here, it seems to me, in the development of Laurel, that we miss the rich comprehensiveness which enhances Miss Welty's earlier work. Laurel's own past pales beside that of her mother. With her parents dead and the house now the property of Fay, only the bridesmaids—her girlhood friends—remain as a remnant of community, and the alcoholic and usually confused Major Bullock is the last repository of myth. In other words Laurel has nothing to sustain her, and she seeks fruitlessly for some relic out of what her life used to be to support her in the present.

Near the end of the novel, after a night of storm and the appearance of a swallow in the house—a symbol of regeneration perhaps, but to what remains doubtful—Laurel seizes upon a breadboard her husband made for her mother and which Fay has defaced by using it to crack walnuts. The imagery is organic and clear: the disparate elements of Laurel's past join in this work of her husband's hands, and for a moment Laurel is almost ready to fight Fay for possession of it. But it is the dream, the memory, not the board which count. Content to leave behind physical reminders of what might have been, Laurel relinquishes the board and except for her departure the story is finished.

What I would point out to you concerning this book is how aesthetically it fulfills the high standards of Miss Welty's earlier work and at the same time disappoints us in the poverty of its conclusion. Laurel wonders if life is worth the pain, and the memory of her husband reassures her. Speaking through the intervening years, he asserts that living with all its difficulties repays the effort. So it does, we may all agree, but we have come to expect much more than this from Miss Welty. The difference between the end of *The Optimist's Daughter* and the final chapter of *The Golden Apples* reflects the difference not between what Miss Welty was capable of twenty years ago and what she can do now, but rather the circumstances under which she writes. The postmodern world with its loss of community and myth will no longer support her.

It is perhaps unfair to balance the picture of Perseus holding the head of Medusa, which illuminates the end of *The Golden Apples*, against the breadboard which Laurel's husband made for Becky—image against image. A better comparison might be the loneliness and even escape of Virgie against the isolation of Laurel. Though at the conclusion of *The Golden Apples* Virgie sits in the rain, her only company an old, and to Virgie strange, black woman, we sense all that is in her past, the richness of the community which has thwarted and sustained her to this moment. She is alone because she *chooses* to be alone and the fact that she *has* a choice makes all the difference. For Laurel, though the game of life is worth the candle, the past remains dead. The community is fragmented and old friendships founder on poor recollection and flawed understanding. On the last night they spend with Laurel, the bridesmaids talk desultorily of their own affairs—husbands and children, marriage and divorce—and when they turn to their common history, they do so inaccurately and without much sympathy. The shared feeling, the kinship have vanished. They speak of Laurel's dead parents, and they laugh without recognizing in their own reminiscences the painful depth of human affection or love's ambiguity.

Laurel sits among her friends, a stranger. In a reversal

of the funeral scene where Major Bullock speaks errone-
ously of Judge McKelva, the bridesmaids remember the
past with accuracy, but they fail quite to comprehend what
things mean. Only Laurel knows that the love between her
mother and father expressed itself and was enriched, as
often as not, by the wrong gift offered and received or the
wrong word spoken. Laurel is isolated, alone, not by
choice, but because she has been thrust there by the erosion of common belief and community. She cannot remain in Mount Salus: her return to her exile in Chicago is
ordained by her own history and the descent of the modern South into fragmentation.

If Miss Welty's work suffers from a contemporary setting,
what of those writers who come after her? Think, for
example, of Flannery O'Connor, a scant sixteen years
younger than Eudora Welty, but who nevertheless had to
work out for herself values and attitudes that Miss Welty
could take for granted. As we know, the decline of myth
and the dissolution of community are accompanied by a
weakening of moral certitude. If we cease to believe in
God, then we lose our sense of transcendent reality, which
in turn means the loss of absolutes. Our ethical structures
are obliterated: principles of right and wrong shade into
each other: each human action becomes a problem that
has to be figured out on its own terms by a process that we
call situation ethics. Let me depart from my immediate
subject for a moment in order to suggest what this state of
affairs means to literature.

Two of the greatest novels of the nineteenth century

were written about adulterous women: *Madame Bovary* and *Anna Karenina*. Each of these women is brought first to misery and then to suicide by her violation of her marriage vows. Both books proceed on the basic assumption, held generally by nineteenth-century society, that adultery is a sin and that the wages of sin is death. Were Flaubert and Tolstoy alive today, the possibilities of their writing these great novels under the present moral climate would be very slim indeed. In an age when journalists in the popular press seriously discuss the advantages of living in sin as opposed to those of living in holy wedlock, we can hardly expect our society to support a work of art that constructs a near tragedy around a woman who grows tired of one man and goes to cohabit with another. Yet the cultural and moral support of his own society is one of the artist's most pressing, if not indispensable, needs.

Flannery O'Connor lived and wrote through the very last years of a southern culture that was literarily viable. Her work was southern, as she never grew tired of proclaiming, and many of the characters and events which appear in her fiction are drawn from life in Milledgeville and at the O'Connor farm, Andalusia. But her work is essentially grotesque, which means that its distorted world exists outside a conventional social context. For the characters in her novels—Haze Moats, young Tarwater— the city is a kind of limbo, symbolic of the negative quality of evil. But the city is not fully described, and her books are thus deprived of one of the traditional resources of the novel—the conveyed sense of life in a specific time and place, the enveloping action. Occasionally, as in

"The Displaced Person,"[3] the world of the farm, the fictional milieu is sketched in with sufficient realism to add depth and scope to the symbolic values of the story, but most of her exaggerated southern types seek their fates against backgrounds as foreign to ordinary life as those of El Greco.

"The Displaced Person" is a splendid accomplishment, and here the Protestant South and Roman Catholicism, that foreign religion, are held in a terrible balance that results at last in characteristically violent death. Mr. Guizac, the Pole, who represents theology, the unvitiated faith, is triumphant at the end, dying as he does, fortified by the last sacraments. But the story is heavily dependent on the Shortleys, the Negroes, Mrs. McIntyre and Mrs. McIntyre's farm, the fields and woods, the barns and the animals. Mr. Guizac does seem in a way to be an abstraction. He is kept at a distance, largely separated from the reader to the end of the story: his humanity is less intense than that of the other, more familiar figures. On the other hand the southern scene, the southern people are concrete, but they are deformed by the failure of their fragmented theology. Only the priest who participates fully in both traditions is whole: it is he who sees the Christ in man and recognizes the transcendent in the beauty of the peacocks. It is clear that without the southern element neither the priest as Miss O'Connor drew him nor the story could exist.

The same can be said, though perhaps to a lesser extent, of *Wise Blood* and of all the stories in *A Good Man Is Hard to Find*. They are more dependent on the southern scene and southern imagery than one might notice at first reading. With *The Violent Bear It Away*, and increasingly with the stories in *Everything That Rises Must Converge*, Miss O'Connor's work became less southern, less dependent on the South as locale and more concerned with her quarrel against the modern world and its prevailing temper, which she took to be destructively gnostic. More and more the catalytic elements in her fiction were intellectual and moral aberrations from beyond the South: Asbury's Zen Buddhism in "The Enduring Chill"; the Wellesley student in "Revelation"; the procrustean psychological theory that infects both Rayber in *The Violent Bear It Away* and Sheppard in "The Lame Shall Enter First." Even the indigenous figures in such stories as "Greenleaf" and "Everything That Rises" are only titularly southern: separated from all tradition, they participate as fully as any northerner or Frenchman in the destructive self-sufficiency of our age.

Calculating, as we must, from the dates that her works were published, the turn in Flannery O'Connor's career came in 1955. After that time there were no more strictly southern stories such as "A Good Man Is Hard to Find" and "The Artificial Nigger" and "The Life You Save May Be Your Own." That Miss O'Connor's career should have entered a second phase is a tribute to her range as a writer, a testament to her deepening wisdom and increasing technical proficiency. But it is interesting also to note how rapidly the country and her section of it were changing during the fifteen years between 1949 when Flannery O'Connor began to publish and 1964 when she died. One of the final measures of her genius, the aspect of her talent that never failed her, was her eye for the cheap and the

obscene and the spurious, no matter under what guises
they presented themselves, no matter where or under
whose auspices they occurred. She saw the tragic polariza-
tion of our contemporary agonies and she displayed them
for us as they sadly developed, but in her own style, drawn
larger than they were, made more absurd.

We know why she wrote as she did. She fully understood
the consequences of the loss of a sense of transcendent
mystery that had overtaken the South as well as the rest of
the world. She used what she could of her southern background, and she used it very well. Caroline Gordon
has remarked that her dialogue is better, more accurate,
than Faulkner's,[4] and in a way this is true. She captures the
syntax, the vocabulary, even the intonations of rural
southern speech so absolutely that her dialogue becomes
an element of the grotesque in its unrelieved singularity.
Robert Fitzgerald refers to her gift for "cartooning."[5] She
spoke of drawing in heavy lines for an audience that was
largely blind in a moral sense.[6]

To put all this another way, strict Christian that she was,
she attempted to furnish for herself and for her work the
consciousness of metaphysical and moral reality that was
missing from the society around her. Understanding fully
that literature is a moral art and comprehending equally
well that the usages of morality and even the recognition
of the moral quality of life had fallen generally into de-
suetude, she attempted to fill out the missing dimension
from her own resources. She did the best that she could
and succeeded better than we had any right to expect. Her
writing achieves the status of art and her voice is distinc-

tive. For instance, that most famous of all her stories, "A Good Man Is Hard to Find," dramatizes a powerful statement about the nature of good and evil. Both the grandmother and the Misfit are intended to be examples of what Miss O'Connor called "good under construction." "Most of us have learned to be dispassionate about evil," she wrote, "but good is another matter. Few have stared at that long enough to accept the fact that its face too is grotesque."[7] She took violence to be a means of grace, one of the methods God uses to get our attention. Seen in this way, the murder of an entire family can be redemptive.

With the loss of God everything else falls out of kilter. Man's knowledge of himself becomes distorted, and he must be reminded even of his own mortality. Old Tarwater, lying in his casket at the beginning of *The Violent Bear It Away*, calls the attention of the modern world to death seen in a Christian context, and how else could this be achieved except through comedy? Other scenes are less successful. Asbury at the end of "The Enduring Chill"[8] discerns in a stain on the wallpaper an image of the Holy Ghost, but the effect is one of contrivance. In general Miss O'Connor was not as profound and finished an artist as Faulkner or Miss Welty, and I am aware that we can never with certainty know why. But I suggest that time had run out on her. Her resources were strained by the deterioration of myth and community, and her energies were drained by the intensity of her argument with a faithless world.

An even better example of the deleterious effect of modern culture on southern literature can be seen in the work of Walker Percy. Nine years older than Miss O'Connor, Percy came late to the pursuit of fiction and did not publish his first novel until 1962. But he got off to a good start with *The Moviegoer*,[9] and though the two writers are vastly different in many respects, he possesses certain views and gifts in common with Miss O'Connor. He too is a Roman Catholic, though a convert, and he has a talent for comedy which he uses to disclose some of the ironies and discrepancies of contemporary man's world view. To this point he and Miss O'Connor travel generally the same road. But Percy is an existentialist. His philosophical heroes are Kierkegaard and Gabriel Marcel, and he shares the prevalent intellectual concern with questions of identity and alienation and malaise.[10]

Binx Bolling, who is the moviegoer, is unable to authenticate his own experience. Moments of high drama that he has seen and lived vicariously in films are more real for him than the events of his own existence. Only when he lay wounded in Korea and thus was brought to the crisis of near death did he encounter life in its deepest manifestations. This is old stuff, made fresh by Percy's wit and the charm with which he has endowed his character. Further the existentialism of *The Moviegoer* is rendered southern by the New Orleans setting, the dialogue, the orientation of the characters. I believe *The Moviegoer* remains the best of Percy's novels in that it comes closest to reconciling the apparent meaninglessness of human existence, seen in the context of its own limitations, with the larger view of man's fate which is held by the pious characters in the book. Binx is saved from the general malaise by the example of his crippled younger brother, who offers his suffering as a prayer for Binx and accepts death cheerfully. As Binx comes to understand, the escape from existential nothingness is effected by the suppression of self, the subordination of individual desire to the altruistic love of another being. Binx marries his cousin Kate, who hovers at the edge of mental disintegration. We are to assume that his love and care for her will continue him in good health as well as rescue her from the modern sickness.

The Moviegoer was a solid beginning for Percy. It encountered the question of modern existence on its own terms and discovered a satisfactory answer. But from this moment Percy's work moved farther and farther away from reality. For Binx the problem is not one of discernment; he knows the difference between fantasy and facts; he simply finds one more interesting, more significant than the other and his problem is to get his experiential mechanisms back in order. Will Barrett, the hero of Percy's second novel *The Last Gentleman*,[11] endures a more serious degree of alienation. At the opening of the novel he is a shaky graduate of a nerve clinic, and his principal concern is to deal with life on its most abecedarian terms: his task is to hold himself together, against events large or small and his own reaction to them.

The Last Gentleman suffers from a good many faults. The characters are not so well drawn as those in *The Moviegoer*; the novel loses focus from too-frequent shifts of scene; the story line is weak and the ending fails to convince us. The point I wish to make, however, is that in his second novel, Percy moves not into, but out of his own culture. The very nature of Barrett's sickness is an inability to distinguish between what is real and what is fanciful. He is separated not only from his past—why, he wonders, does he lack the moral certainty of his forebears—but from his present as well. He does not know who or what he is; he is ignorant of the terms of his own existence; he is modern man, alone in the crowd and his sphere of action is hardly larger than his brain pan.

Such a rendition of the plight of contemporary human beings may well be accurate, but what I am trying to sketch for you is the impoverishment of southern fiction under a new dispensation. Whatever else we may say about it, southern fiction in order to be southern fiction must take its main ground in the South and concern itself with southern culture, southern habits and beliefs, southern people. The thrust of my argument is that literature dies as the culture which supports it dies, and I have attempted to show in this chapter how the diminishing strength and growing fragmentation of traditional southern civilization dilute the enveloping action of Eudora Welty's most recent work and deprive Flannery O'Connor of a proper context for her narratives. In his latest novel Walker Percy takes the final step: *Love in the Ruins*[12] is set in the future.

Fantasy is in vogue these days, and serious critics are giving serious attention to science fiction. It is easy to see why this should be so. Realistic literature of every sort languishes, and I speak now not only of the South but of the Western world in general. Every year new talents appear, to be praised and then to be forgotten. Promise is almost never fulfilled: careers move downhill: novelists turn away from art in favor of journalism. The old forms and formulas cease to work, and the artist looks for new techniques and new subject matter. Underneath all this lies at best a distrust of—at worst a destructive animosity toward—contemporary culture. In a brilliant essay, "Spatial Form in Modern Literature," first published in 1945, Joseph Frank, following the German critic Wilhelm Worringer, proves conclusively that art through the ages has been more or less realistic (or representational) in proportion to society's satisfaction with its own historical and cultural and metaphysical situation. Well-ordered and confident civilizations produce art that reflects as closely as possible the physical surroundings and the circumstances of human existence. In cultures afflicted with doubt and uncertainty, art tends toward abstraction as the artist and the society seek to turn away from an environment which they find distasteful or even frightening. Frank concludes: "The objective historical imagination, on which modern man has prided himself . . . , is transformed in these writers into the mythical imagination for which historical time does not exist. . . . This timeless world of myth, forming the common content of modern literature, . . . finds its appropriate esthetic expression in spatial form."[13] The point is that as southern fiction has become more affected by modernism, it has increasingly moved away from the metaphysical myth which arose from the common experience of the South into a poetic myth which is by turns gnostic or utopian. The crisis of civilization in the nation as a whole has adversely influenced southern writing. The novelist now moves forward—not backward—into time. This is the ultimate denial of history.

So Percy, unwilling or unable to deal with the present, moves his fictional construct a few years ahead and intimates that the end of the world is upon us. I do not want to dwell on *Love in the Ruins*, for it seems to me that like most works that attempt to depict what lies ahead, the novel is lacking in imaginative power. The trouble is that because human beings have limited intelligence, we see the future, but not very clearly. History always has a trick up its sleeve, and consequently a simple extrapolation of present miseries into future catastrophes fails to tell enough of the truth. But this is the line Percy follows. In the southern part of the United States in 1983, most tertiary industry has ceased to function. Unrepaired automobiles litter the streets; abandoned buildings crumble under the sun; lawns are uncut, meals are unserved, floors are unvacuumed. The breakdown of society continues along familiar vectors. Militant blacks live in the swamp and launch occasional raids on white subdivisions. Alienated youth—some of them past thirty—occupy an island. The church is split into liberal and conservative and centrist groups; abortion and euthanasia have become respectable medical procedures. The government continues to expand its bureaucracy. The care of the aged is a vexing problem.

I recognize the satirical element here, but Percy has no norm against which to measure our present and future excesses. His physician hero is as disoriented, as afflicted with the modern malaise, as the next man. Unable to heal himself, he broods over the fate he shares with the rest of humanity and devises finally a miraculous machine by means of which individuals can be cured of their anxieties and have their personalities reintegrated. This is a lovely dream and for a while Percy writes as though he means to adhere to it. But of course no such machine really exists, and Percy takes his art too seriously to contrive his plot and manipulate his characters in terms of an ontological lapsometer. He concludes with his familiar theme that we should love and care for each other. But the fact that he would set his novel in the future and traffic with scientific magic—even in a satirical vein—is indicative of his divorce as an artist from his own culture.

Yet, as mixed a performance as I consider *Love in the Ruins* to be, I want to give Percy his due. His despair and his literary defects emerge from a sense of loss, a decent concern with what might have been and what might be still if only we could find an answer. Torn as he is between science and religion, hearing with his sensitive ear all the competing claims of our fragmented world, he attempts to walk a middle road which continually disintegrates beneath him. But he stands firmly on the side of life and thus distinguishes himself in an age fraught with madness. In *The Use and Abuse of Art* Jacques Barzun extends Worringer's thesis and shows how, beginning in the last century, the main stream of artistic endeavor has been consistent in its effort to destroy the world. In its naturalistic excesses art has made war on nature, which is to say on the very created order of the universe. In the service of ideology, art has made war on various classes of society—the bourgeois, the aristocracy—and on the systems by which men arrange their lives. But in the destruction of nature and society, art itself is destroyed.[14]

Let me give you an example taken from the literature of the South. One of the most promising novelists to appear in recent years is Cormac McCarthy whose first book won the William Faulkner Award and was praised by such critics as Malcolm Cowley and Robert Penn Warren. McCarthy is extremely talented. His prose, though reminiscent of Faulkner, is clean and sharply detailed. His characters come immediately alive. He has a fine sense of dramatic scene and pacing and an ability to reproduce the countryside of east Tennessee where his fiction is set. In *The Orchard Keeper*[15] he pursues a familiar theme: he charts the depredations of time and shows how old ways are doomed by the new. No southern novelist since William Styron has got off to a better start. But in his second book,[16] McCarthy told a weird, almost gothic tale of incest and his third novel is clear evidence of the plane of madness to which our art has finally descended.

The name of McCarthy's novel is *Child of God*,[17] which can be taken as a kind of blasphemous irony. Flannery O'Connor points out that one method of discrediting God is to charge Him with the suffering of the innocent.[18] Another device, equally destructive, is to celebrate, out of any context of the totality of creation, the most depraved instincts of mankind. McCarthy's child of God is Lester Ballard who, having been dispossessed of his land for failure to pay his taxes, releases his angry and degenerate mentality upon the world. He is a voyeur and in pursuit of this pastime he comes upon a couple dead from carbon monoxide in the back seat of an automobile. Ballard pushes aside the body of the man and violates the body of the woman. Then he takes the female corpse back to the shack where he is living, buys clothes for her, makes up her face with rouge and lipstick. But even in winter time, bodies do not last, so Ballard turns to murder in order to keep himself supplied with corpses on which to practice his necrophilia. At the end of the novel we find him living in a cave which is generously furnished with cadavers of both sexes.

The scant outline that I offer here can in no way suggest the brutal horror of McCarthy's novel. Our talents are available to us, whatever use we choose to make of them, and McCarthy tells Ballard's story with extraordinary skill. If we regard the book from a purely literary perspective, judging it on how nearly and skillfully it fulfills its intentions, then beyond question we must call the novel a success. In these terms Anatole Broyard has praised *Child of God* as manifesting an art that "hath charms to soothe the indignant breast."[19] In spite of all the effective writing and the generation of dramatic tension, it is not a consummated work of art but an affront to decency on every level. Thus it confounds many of our modern theories about the sanctity of the artist and the methods by which we should gauge his work. But I stray from my theme. McCarthy and his writing constitute the best, but by no means the only, example I can find of that destructive impulse in contemporary art of which Barzun reminds us. Unlike the other writers whose work I have discussed in this chapter, McCarthy is the artist not merely bereft of community and myth; he has declared war against these ancient repositories of order and truth. One should not think of him as simply an extreme instance of evil that has always existed in the world. Instead one should see him as a portent of the barbarism that even now begins to engulf the world. This novel confirms a pattern of sensationalism and decadence in the southern novel which extends from Erskine Caldwell through Carson McCullers and James Dickey to McCarthy. The mode might properly be called grotesque local color.

I do not wish to close on this note of pessimism. At the end of *Love in the Ruins* Percy's main character has found a way to survive the defects of his crumbling civilization. After a life of infidelities and excesses he has married and settled down to raise children and to work in his garden. He has resumed the practice of his religion and intends totally to keep faith with God and his fellow man. What our world needs, Percy has admonished us, are novelists concerned with values not necessarily literary,[20] and I concur with him most heartily: better *Love in the Ruins* with all its flaws than the perfectly rendered depravities that Cormac McCarthy presents.

The protagonist of *Love in the Ruins* is named Thomas More, and in pointing out that he is a collateral descendent of the original bearer of that name, Percy invites us to draw comparisons between the two men, the two societies. The first More was born at the close of the Middle Ages

and died a martyr to the birth pangs of the English Renaissance. He was one of the original humanists, a disciple of
Colet, and intimate of Erasmus, the author of *Utopia;* and
his distinguished political career brought him at last to
the office of lord chancellor. Yet none of the honors and
accomplishments of his life so become his memory and
incite our admiration as his conduct during his trial and
imprisonment and his manner at his execution. By prais-
ing More, I do not mean to recommend to the world at
large the course of martyrdom. Most of us lack both
strength and faith, and we may hope in our weakness to be
deprived also of the opportunity. But I do think that we
might look to More as well as to Percy to seek a guide by
which we might reorder our priorities.

The practice of literature is a mundane pursuit, and
though it is true that art is long and life fleeting, it is equally
true that at the end of all time *Oedipus Rex* and the *Divine
Comedy*, *Hamlet*, and *Light in August* will cease to be along
with the rest of our human paraphernalia. Beginning with
the ascendency of romanticism and increasingly in our
own time, we have come to think too highly of literature.
Barzun reminds us that in the nineteenth century art
supplanted religion in the minds of artists, then in the
minds of their followers, as the revelation of ultimate
truth, the repository of the highest reality. This led to the
aestheticism that reigned between 1890 and 1914, which
in turn set us upon the pernicious road that art follows
today.[21] James Joyce codified the attitude that has pre-
vailed increasingly in artistic and intellectual circles as this

century has progressed. Art replaces God; the artist replaces the priest; the superiority of the artist and his creation to all other people and forms of endeavor are thus established.[22] As Barzun puts it, all persons who are not artists "might as well vacate the premises."[23]

The consequences of this attitude are difficult to exaggerate. As I have already mentioned, nature is denigrated because the artist refuses to imitate her but deals more and more with the abstract forms and structures which he develops out of his own imagination. Human and social constructs, which are based on reality observed in nature and in the natural law suffer the same fate. Worst of all, morality and the transcendent truth from which it derives are subordinated to the amorality of art. Thus Faulkner's statement that the artist will and indeed should rob his grandmother in order to do his work[24] goes virtually unchallenged and is applauded as evidence of a properly serious attitude toward literature. Our indulgence of the artist has caught up with us, and the chaos that we see everywhere around us was bound to ensue.

Finally I would suggest that if literature, in the South or elsewhere, is to survive, we must put the artist in his proper place. We must cease to worship him for his skill, no matter how great that skill may be. For only when we begin to see art as a vocation like and no better than any other can we expect a rejuvenation of our literature. This is true because to comprehend the artistic gift as a simple calling is a first step toward our discovery of new and better manifestations of community and myth.

Notes

Introduction

1. A Yeats manuscript first published by Richard Ellmann. See his *James Joyce* (New York: Oxford University Press, 1959), p. 107.

2. "Aspects of the Southern Philosophy," in *Southern Renascence: The Literature of the Modern South*, ed. Louis D. Rubin, Jr., and Robert D. Jacobs (Baltimore: Johns Hopkins Press, 1953), p. 16.

3. Ellmann (interview with Frank Budgen), *James Joyce*, p. 27.

4. "The Snopes Trilogy," *Sewanee Review* 68 (1960):323–324.

5. "Foreword to *A Novel, a Novella, and Four Short Stories*," *The Hero with the Private Parts* (Baton Rouge: Louisiana State University Press, 1966), p. 194.

6. *The Velvet Horn* (New York: McDowell-Obolensky, 1957), p. 368.

7. "The Gaze Past, the Glance Present," *Memoirs and Opinions* (Chicago: Swallow Press, 1975), p. 36.

8. Paul Schmidt, "Between Book Ends," *St. Louis Post-Dispatch*, August 6, 1959, p. 12.

ONE—*Myth*

1. "Religion and the Old South," *Essays of Four Decades* (Chicago: Swallow Press, 1968), p. 559.

2. "Why the Modern South Has a Great Literature," *Still Rebels, Still Yankees and Other Essays* (Baton Rouge: Louisiana State University Press, 1957), pp. 172–173.

3. "The New Faustus: The Southern Renascence and the Joycean Aesthetic," in *Southern Fiction Today: Renascence and Beyond*, ed. George Core (Athens: University of Georgia Press, 1969), p. 11.

4. *Pale Horse, Pale Rider* (New York: Harcourt, Brace, 1939), p. 4.

5. Ibid., p. 79.

6. Ibid., p. 80.

7. Ibid., pp. 88–89.

8. *Absalom, Absalom!* (New York: Random House, 1936).

9. "The Tragic Design of *Absalom, Absalom!*," *South Atlantic Quarterly* 50 (1951):552–566.

10. *Light in August* (New York: Smith and Haas, 1932).

11. *Essays of Four Decades*, p. 574.

12. "The Southern Recovery of Memory and History," *Sewanee Review* 82 (1974):1–32.

13. Ibid., p. 11.

14. *Cosmos and History: The Myth of the Eternal Return*, trans. Willard Trask (New York: Harper and Brothers, 1959).

15. Ibid., p. 11.

16. *The American Adam: Innocence, Tragedy, and Tradition in the Nineteenth Century* (Chicago: University of Chicago Press, 1955).

17. The Machine in the Garden: Technology and the Pastoral Ideal in America (New York: Oxford University Press, 1964).

18. *All the King's Men* (New York: Harcourt, Brace, 1946).

19. *The Use and Abuse of Art* (Princeton: Princeton University Press, 1974).

20. *All the King's Men*, p. 464.

21. See, for example, Cleanth Brooks, "Religion and Literature," *Sewanee Review* 82 (1974): 93–107.

22. "Southern Writers in the Modern World: Death by Melancholy," *Death by Melancholy: Essays on Modern Southern Fiction* (Baton Rouge: Louisiana State University Press, 1973), pp. 114–130.

23. *The Confessions of Nat Turner* (New York: Random House, 1967).

TWO —*Community*

1. Robert Penn Warren, "Andrew Lytle's *The Long Night:* A Rediscovery," *Southern Review*, n.s. 7 (1971):133.

2. *The Long Night* (Indianapolis: Bobbs-Merrill, 1936), pp. 188–189.

3. The Fathers (New York: G. P. Putnam's Sons, 1938).

4. See, for example, Arthur Mizener's introduction to *The Fathers* (Denver: Alan Swallow, 1962), pp. ix–xix.

5. *The Fathers*, p. 35.

6. Walter Sullivan, "*The Fathers* and the Failure of Tradition," forthcoming in the *Southern Review*.

7. *The Fathers*, p. 306.

8. "Ode to the Confederate Dead," *The Swimmers and Other Selected Poems* (New York: Charles Scribner's Sons, 1970), pp. 17–20.

9. *The Unvanquished* (New York: Random House, 1938).

10. "The Son of Man: He Will Prevail," *The Hero with the Private Parts* (Baton Rouge: Louisiana State University Press, 1966), pp. 103–128.

11. Ibid., p. 123.

12. *The Unvanquished*, p. 249.
13. *Light in August* (New York: Harrison Smith and Robert Haas, 1932).
14. "A Rose for Emily," *These Thirteen* (New York: Jonathan Cape and Harrison Smith, 1931).
15. *The Golden Apples* (New York: Harcourt, Brace, 1949).
16. Ibid., pp. 8–85.
17. Ibid., p. 44.
18. Ibid., p. 79.
19. Ibid., pp. 99–138.
20. Ibid., pp. 203–244.
21. Ibid., pp. 212, 236.
22. Ibid., p. 243.

THREE—*Rainbow's End*

1. "In Time of the Breaking of Nations: The Decline of Southern Fiction," *Death by Melancholy* (Baton Rouge: Louisiana State University Press, 1972), pp. 87–96.
2. *The Fathers* (New York: G. P. Putnam's Sons, 1938), p. 268.
3. *A Good Man Is Hard to Find* (New York: Harcourt, Brace, 1955), pp. 197–251.
4. "Heresy in Dixie," *Sewanee Review* 76 (1968):268.
5. Robert Fitzgerald, Introduction, *Everything That Rises Must Converge* (New York: Farrar, Straus and Giroux, 1965), p. vii.
6. *Mystery and Manners: Occasional Prose*, edited by Sally and Robert Fitzgerald (New York: Farrar, Straus and Giroux, 1969), p. 34.
7. Ibid., p. 266.
8. *Everything That Rises Must Converge*, pp. 82–114.
9. *The Moviegoer* (New York: Knopf, 1961).
10. See Martin Luschei, *The Sovereign Wayfarer: Walker Percy's Diagnosis of the Malaise* (Baton Rouge: Louisiana State University Press, 1972), pp. 19–63 and passim.
11. *The Last Gentleman* (New York: Farrar, Straus and Giroux, 1966).
12. *Love in the Ruins* (New York: Farrar, Straus and Giroux, 1971).
13. "Spatial Form in Modern Literature," *Sewanee Review* 53 (1945):653.
14. *The Use and Abuse of Art* (Princeton: Princeton University Press, 1974), pp. 123–150.
15. *The Orchard Keeper* (New York: Random House, 1965).
16. *Outer Dark* (New York: Random House, 1968).
17. *Child of God* (New York: Random House, 1973)
18. *Mystery and Manners*, pp. 226–227.
19. *Aroused by Books* (New York: Random House, 1974), p. 281.

20. "Notes for a Novel about the End of the World," *The Message in the Bottle: How Queer Man Is, How Queer Language Is, and What One Has to Do with the Other* (New York: Farrar, Straus and Giroux), pp. 101–118.

21. *The Use and Abuse of Art*, pp. 24–46.

22. *A Portrait of the Artist as a Young Man* (New York: Viking Press, 1956).

23. *The Use and Abuse of Art,* p. 18.

24. "An Interview with William Faulkner" by Jean Stein, in *Writers at Work: The Paris Review Interviews*, ed. Malcolm Cowley (New York: Viking Press, 1959), p. 124.

Index